DR.LUKE'S

PRESCRIPTIONS

FOR

SPIRITUAL HEALTH

DR. LUKE'S
PRESCRIPTIONS
FOR
SPIRITUAL HEALTH

THOMAS R. McDANIEL

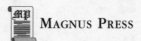

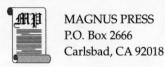

MAGNUS PRESS
P.O. Box 2666
Carlsbad, CA 92018

Dr. Luke's Prescriptions for Spiritual Health

First Edition, 2000

Printed in the United States of America

LCCN: 00-131401
ISBN: 0-9654806-6-6

Publisher's Cataloguing-in-Publication
(Provided by Quality Books, Inc.)

McDaniel, Thomas R.
    Dr. Luke's prescriptions for spiritual health/
by Thomas R. McDaniel -- 1st ed.
    p. cm.
    LCCN: 00-131401
    ISBN: 0-9654806-6-6

    1. Bible. N.T. Luke--Commentaries. 2. Bible N.T. Luke--Criticism, interpretation, etc.
3. Christian life. I. Title

BS2595.3.M33 2000   226.4'06
                     QBI00-337

---

05 04 03 02 01 00   10 9 8 7 6 5 4 3 2 1

DEDICATION

To the Fellowship Class of First Presbyterian Church, Spartanburg, South Carolina. For over a quarter of a century they have taught me, their teacher, many things: discipline, patience, forgiveness—and love.

and

To Nan. You *are* the best.

TABLE OF CONTENTS

PREFACE

Why another book on the Gospel According to Luke? There are many commentaries—some succinct and practical, some long and scholarly—but none organized around the theme of spiritual health. Luke was a physician, the only physician who wrote a book of the Bible, and he saw the message of the "good news" of Jesus through the lens of his personal and professional experience. So it is for all of us. It is possible to gain a new perspective on the gospel by looking at it the way Luke probably did: as a message of hope for a sin-sick world.

For Luke, as a physician, the central question of life was, "how can people lead healthy lives?" The physician-as-gospel-writer found in the words and deeds of Jesus a "power-full" antidote for broken humanity: the poor, the sick, the afflicted, the deranged, the lost, and the misguided. Jesus, given God's power by the Holy Spirit, brought to the suffering a message of spiritual hope and health by the twin medicines of faith and love. As Luke records one pronouncement of Jesus, "It is not the healthy who need a doctor, but the sick" (5:31).

But who is sick? In one way or another *everyone*. For this reason Luke's lovely Gospel provides provocative prescriptions for any person—in ancient times or today—choosing to follow the path of wellness to eternal life. Consequently, Luke's Gospel is indeed the universal good news for all people. And it is for contemporary Christians also a medical alert. May this special perspective on the Gospel According to Luke bring you a richer spiritual life and a healthier soul.

Acknowledgements

I am indebted to many friends and colleagues who have provided encouragement, constructive criticism, and assistance during the development and publication of this book.

My pastors Dr. Jim Fogartie and Dr. Todd Jones, and my physician friends Dr. Tom Roberts and Dr. Mac Davis gave me encouragement and expertise in matters theological and medical. Gladys Jackson, Don MacArthur, and Nan McDaniel provided sound advice based on their close reading of early drafts. My able assistant Debra Young cheerfully endured countless revisions and gave me excellent word processing at every stage of writing. Dr. Byron McCane, a professor in our Department of Religion and Philosophy at Converse College, also contributed useful suggestions that have improved my analysis of Luke's Gospel with the special emphasis on spiritual health.

Finally, I want to express my appreciation to Warren Angel and the fine editorial staff at Magnus for taking on this project and bringing it to a successful completion. Every book is a partnership between an author and a publisher, and this partnership has been a pleasure.

CHAPTER 1

AN INTRODUCTION TO LUKE AND HIS GOSPEL

"The health of a nation is measured
by how it treats those on the margin."
—Chuck Colson

Health. What exactly is it? Everyone wants it. Volumes have been written about how to achieve it and how to keep it. Is it the absence of illness? Or something more? Do doctors hold the key to good health? Or someone else? How important is the "patient" in the fight against disease? What is the relationship of mind, body, and spirit in the health equation? Does the Bible offer prescriptions for spiritual health? And what exactly is "spiritual health"? In our modern quest for health—wellness, if you prefer—we can turn to the New Testament for help. There, Christians will find insights. And wisdom. And advice.

The Gospel According to Luke is an extraordinary source of Biblical wisdom on the topic of health. That should be no real surprise. Everyone knows that Luke—who wrote more pages of the New Testament than any other single individual—was a physician, as far as we know the only medical authority to pen a book of the Bible. Furthermore, he was probably the only Gentile to write for the Holy Book. Some scholars dispute Luke's role as a physician and contend that the medical language in this gospel would have been mastered by any well-educated Greek of his day. However, internal evidence in the text points to his medical role.

Although not a famous figure in the early church, he was known to be a faithful companion of Paul—who called him in

Colossians 4:14 "the beloved physician." He may have served as a ship's doctor on Paul's missionary journeys. Like Paul, he no doubt developed a deep personal belief in the power of Christ to forgive sins and redeem the sinner through total faith in Him as the Savior of the world. For Christians, then as now, only by faith can the believer be transformed, resurrected, born again to perfect health—and life eternal. So, modern reader, consider how the ancient physician understood and applied the gospel as an extended set of prescriptions for a healthy life. Think of him as your personal physician while you undertake your own missionary journey, wherever that takes you in our complex world today.

Luke was not only a physician and a Gentile but an excellent historian and, according to legend, a skilled painter. He was what a later age might call a Renaissance Man, steeped in philosophy and literature and proficient as a man of thought and action. His Greek is elegant and poetic, and his experience included extended academic studies as well as considerable travel. Some authorities speculate that he might have studied medicine at the university in Tarsus, perhaps even meeting Paul and Apollos during his student days. Some scholars think he may have studied at the University of Berytus or the University of Laodicea (where a particularly fine medical school was located). In any event, it was normal for first-century Greek physicians to be highly educated in literature as well as medicine. In all likelihood he lived in Macedonia and, some say, might early in life have been a slave later freed by his owner, Theophilus, to whom both Luke and Acts are addressed.

There are many guides, scholarly works, and commentaries for the reader who wants an in-depth understanding of the book of Luke. I have relied on these sources of insight and interpretation as I have focused on the theme of Dr. Luke's prescriptions for spiritual health. My own interest in this theme grew out of a combination of factors: as an educator, I am committed to understanding how academic disciplines arrive at truths; as an elder in the Presbyterian Church and a

long-time teacher of an adult Sunday school class, I am inter-
ested in Bible study; as a middle-aged man with the normal
concerns our age group has for diet, blood pressure, and
peace of mind, I have all of our contemporary fascinations
with "wellness" and a healthy life style. Consequently, my
recent determination to examine Luke's rendition of the
gospel has contributed much to my personal and spiritual
growth. I think of this venture as an exploration in the education of a soul. May it be so for you.

What else might be useful in this brief introduction?
About the book of Luke, you might want to note these
features:

- It is the longest of the four Gospels in terms of words
  (Matthew has more *chapters*), and along with Acts consti-
  tutes about one-fourth of the New Testament.

- It is a Gospel written especially for the non-Jewish reader,
  tracing Jesus' genealogy not to Abraham but to Adam—
  the father of the human race.

- It is a Gospel with the message of universal salvation, for
  the Gentile as well as the Jew and for the sinner as well as
  the saint.

- It is a Gospel of prayer and praise, containing the great
  hymns of praise: the *Magnificat, Benedictus,* and *Nunc
  Dimittis.*

- It is a Gospel giving special attention to life's outcasts:
  women, sinners, and the poor (those "on the margin").

- It is a Gospel presented as a careful interpretive history to
  give the noble Theophilus ("lover of God") an "orderly
  account" of Jesus' life and work.

- It is a Gospel reflecting the humanitarian's concern for
  family and social welfare.

- It is a Gospel reflecting the physician's concern for the
  human illnesses of body, mind, and spirit.

As William Barclay notes so astutely, "a minister sees men

at their best, a lawyer sees men at their worst, and a doctor sees men as they are." Dr. Luke saw men and women as human beings in need of the healing power of the gospel of love.

And about Dr. Luke—scientist, historian, artist, philosopher, Christian convert—you might want to note these additional observations:

- Luke may have been a Syrian by birth, hailing from the city of Antioch on the Mediterranean.

- Luke accompanied Paul on his Second Journey across the Aegean from Troas in Asia Minor to Philippi in Greece, his Third Journey six years later from Philippi to Jerusalem, and his final journey from Caesarea to Rome.

- Luke was an early member of the Christian community in Antioch, where much of the early history of Christianity developed as a mission to the Gentiles.

- Luke, some documents report, was unmarried, wrote his Gospel in Greece, and died at the age of 84.

- Luke might have written his Gospel before A.D. 64 (he makes no reference to Paul's martyrdom in that year) or after A.D. 70 (he seems to describe—rather than predict— the fall of Jerusalem in that year).

- Luke emphasizes the power of the Holy Spirit and complements his portrayal of Jesus' gracious humanity with a strong sense of the supernatural.

- Luke alone presents the parables of the Prodigal Son and the Good Samaritan—and the account of the shepherds who came to Bethlehem at the time of Jesus' birth.

Our focus, however, will be on Luke the physician and on how his experience as a doctor allowed him to understand the life and message of Jesus as a call to healthy living—and repentance from the sins that lead to illness, disease, and death.

While scholars do not know a great deal about Luke's medical education, some of his knowledge is manifested directly in his Gospel.* Luke often uses the specific medical terms in vogue among Greek physicians of the first-century. For example, when Jesus raised Jairus' daughter and said "get up little girl" and then added that she got up "at once," Luke describes this event with clinical terms. Then he adds that Jesus ordered some food for her, a common prescription in Greek medical practice of the time. When Luke describes the difficulty for a camel to pass through the eye of a needle, he uses the Greek word for a *surgical* needle. When Jesus cures Simon's mother-in-law of a fever, Luke uses the medical term for a "high fever," probably typhus.

In many other instances we see Luke's keen interest in medicine in evidence while other Gospel writers are less precise, less technical, and less clinical. Luke reports illnesses representing different categories of disease or affliction. So, while Matthew reports five separate cases where Jesus healed a blind man and three cases where he healed a deaf person, Luke gives an account of only one case (in more detail) in each category. By choosing representative cases, he shows us something of his scientific approach to the gospel.

We must always remember that Luke, like most physicians educated in first-century Greece, was as much a philosopher as a scientist. To be effective, the Greeks held, physicians needed to understand the total human experience and to see illness within the broadest possible context. Medicine was not regarded as mere technique—body mechanics—but as the application of wisdom to the solution of problems that were physical, mental, moral, social, and spiritual. In some ways, the ancient Greek philosophy of medicine is similar to contemporary movements toward "holistic medicine" and "wellness." It is in this sense that we will be looking at applications of Luke's medical wisdom for arriving at "spiritual health."

As Luke brought together his understanding of medicine and his new-found faith in Christ, he came to see spiritual health as the work of a "quintessential" force in the lives of

---

* For an interesting discussion of this contention, see Werner G. Marx, "Luke, the Physician Re-examined," Expository Times, Vol. 91, March 1980, pp. 168-172.

people of faith. From his exclusive account of the conception by Mary to his compelling accounts of Jesus' healing work, Luke tells us much of the human condition—spiritual as well as physical. For Luke wellness was ultimately the work of a powerful force for health: the Holy Spirit of God.

In this book, I have concentrated on Luke's Gospel as a guide for spiritual health. Each chapter addresses this theme in terms of a particular dimension of human experience: physical, mental, moral, financial, and religious. I contend that "spiritual health" embraces all these dimensions. The person who is spiritually healthy has learned how to live the integrated life—a life of *integrity*. Spiritually healthy individuals are at peace with themselves and their fellow humans. They have minimized (or, better yet, reconciled) the conflicts within and without. They have unified the elements of their personal and social lives in a way that makes them "whole." That is what the Greek word for *health* literally means. Most of all, they will have come to understand the joy of new life promised by Jesus to all who profess the faith that frees people to serve and love.

Luke knew this as well as anyone in his age—or ours. He penned his Gospel account to give his readers (Theophilus and us) the "good news" that the Holy Spirit of God, incarnate in Christ, is the source of peace, unity, and health. He declares in his prologue that his purpose for writing was to provide an "orderly account," a true and integrated story of Jesus' message and ministry. In this way, Luke begins his task with wholeness as his Gospel's criterion. Should we be surprised, then, that Luke sees the gospel message itself as a call for, and a prescription for, spiritual health?

It is true, as Chuck Colson contends, that "the health of a nation is measured by how it treats those on the margin." We might do well to admit that *all* of us are on that margin. How do we minister to the health needs of all of us? Let us look at Luke's Gospel with this special perspective on health. May the insights, wisdom, and advice herein serve you as prescriptions for a happier, more satisfying, healthier life.

CHAPTER 2

PHYSICAL HEALTH

*"It is much more important to know
what sort of patient has a disease than to know
what kind of disease a patient has."*
—William Osler

As Luke begins his Gospel, a "connected narrative" to give Theophilus "authentic knowledge" about the ministry of Jesus (1:1-4, NEB), he introduces us (as well as Theophilus) to the remarkable physical and spiritual births of John the Baptist and Jesus. The angel Gabriel tells John's father, Zechariah, that Elizabeth and he would have a son even though she was barren and both parents-to-be were well on in years. The son, John, would "never touch wine or strong drink," and "even before his birth he will be filled with the Holy Spirit" (1:15). For Mary the birth of a son was to be even more amazing. As she told Gabriel, "How can this be, since I am a virgin?" (1:34). But, again, the power of the Holy Spirit would provide the miraculous special blessing.

So, from the outset of his Gospel account, Luke makes clear his conviction that the Holy Spirit—the breath of God—was moving in the lives of the faithful to produce marvelous physical consequences. And marvelous spiritual consequences, too. For Luke it is always the *pneuma* of God, the Holy Spirit, which produces the most vital lives, lives characterized by unrivaled spiritual health. Although John and Jesus—cousins born six months apart—were quite different people, each approached living with a kind of energy and life force that would change the world. John would be a Nazirite, living a holy life in the wilderness, eating locusts and wild honey, growing "strong in spirit," and preaching a message of judgment and repentance; Jesus would grow "strong, filled with wisdom," preaching a message of love and forgiveness.

John and Jesus: two healthy young men of faith given power by the Holy Spirit from their very conceptions to help a sin-sick world regain spiritual health.

"Full of the Holy Spirit," Jesus withstood the temptations of Satan and began his work in Galilee. His very first teaching in the synagogue on the Sabbath addressed the text in Isaiah that reads: "The Spirit of the Lord is upon me...; he has anointed me to bring good news to the poor. . . to proclaim release to the captives and recovery of sight to the blind, to let the oppressed go free..." (4:18-19). For Luke, Jesus' message of spiritual power, good news, and physical healing was the fundamental prescription of the gospel. Forgiveness and love would be the spiritual medicine he would bring to the world's broken victims. Who are these victims and what ailments do they bring to Jesus? How do various patients respond to Jesus' prescriptions?

Examples of Physical Healing

Luke describes how, during the early years of his ministry, Jesus healed many diseases and physical afflictions, always with unusual authority and power. Consider some examples Luke describes, remembering his practice of selecting representative cases to demonstrate a variety of ailments and the range of Jesus' healing power.

One of the first cures Jesus provided for a physical problem was for Simon's mother-in-law, who, Luke says, was "suffering from a high fever" (4:38-39). Jesus came "and stood over her and rebuked the fever, and it left her. Immediately she got up and began to serve them." Because Luke uses the medical language of his day, we can be sure that this woman was definitely laid up with a major illness. The Greeks divided fevers into two classifications—high and low or major and minor—and a high fever might well have been typhus.

This illness would test Jesus' powers more than a "low" or "minor" fever such as malaria. Jesus was quick to respond to the illness, "rebuked the fever," and Simon's mother-in-law was cured at once. Perhaps as significant as the cure is the woman's response: "She got up at once and waited on them," an apparent sign of her gratitude.

On another occasion soon after, Jesus encountered a leper who "bowed with his face to the ground" and begged his help (5:12). At that time, the worst form of leprosy was considered to be so highly contagious that sufferers were required to separate themselves from the healthy and to publicly declare themselves "unclean." As with fevers, the Greek physicians divided leprosy into two categories: mild and severe. The social stigma for lepers could be personally devastating, for leprosy was both a physical and social disease. The person suffering from it was a total outcast.

But Luke tells us that Jesus, unafraid, reached out in love and healing power and "touched him." And when his hand went out to this man no one dared come near, his skin cleared up "immediately" (5:13). Jesus instructed the leper to make the offering required by Moses to "certify the cure."

Jesus' reputation as a physician preceded him wherever he went. Luke says that "many crowds gathered to hear him and to be cured of their ailments" (5:15). Jesus cured the multitudes—and from time to time "he would withdraw to deserted places and pray" (5:16). Where did Jesus get his extraordinary power and authority to heal the sick? For Luke, the answer is clear: from the Holy Spirit. At his baptism in the Jordan River, "the Holy Spirit descended upon him in bodily form like a dove" (3:22). Jesus would later announce in the synagogue at Nazareth, "The Spirit of the Lord is upon me, because he has anointed me to bring good news to the poor." (4:18). And Jesus spent hours upon hours alone with God in prayer. This too gave him strength and guidance in Spirit-filled ministry.

But cures required something from the patient too.

The patient's contribution to renewed health is effectively

illustrated by the well-known incident of the paralytic. Some friends of the paralytic brought him to Jesus. The crowds had grown so large by this time that the friends could not get close to the master healer. So, they took the paralytic, bed and all, to the roof and let him down through an open space. Luke records that Jesus took notice: "When he saw their faith he said, 'Friend, your sins are forgiven you' " (5:20).

Luke knows that healing comes from the Holy Spirit. In this case, the friends' faith became the instrument of access to God's *pneuma*. The healing work of the Holy Spirit requires the willing and active participation of the patient but responds, too, to the faith of one's companions. Luke says that the patient stood up "immediately," took up his bed, and "went home, glorifying God" (5:25).

Now, this healing was performed in the presence of the Pharisees and the scribes. The Pharisees emerged as leaders in the time of the Maccabees, and the scribes go back at least to Ezra in the post-exilic period. Together, they were the guardians of Jewish law. These religious leaders and lawyers were building a case against Jesus as a blasphemer and a breaker of religious laws. Only God can forgive sins, they said, and Jesus blasphemes—a capital crime—when he presumes to forgive the paralytic's sins. But what does sin have to do with affliction?

The religious orthodoxy of Judaism assumed that bodily afflictions were deserved punishments for sin. Recall the remonstrance from Job's counselor friends as they put forth explanations for Job's suffering. Eliphaz tells Job, "the wicked writhe in pain all their days" (Job 15:20). Later he advises, "Agree with God, and be at peace" (Job 22:21). Another friend, Elihu, reminds Job that God's justice requires "that man learns his lesson on a bed of pain, tormented by a ceaseless ague in his bones" (Job 33:19, NEB). In the context of such thinking about sin and sickness, Luke observed the contrasting attitudes of Jesus and the Pharisees. The Pharisees justified illness as a proper consequence of sin; Jesus cured illness because God prefers us to be well. How like the Pharisees are we when we ask, "what did I do to deserve my illness?"

For much of the rest of Luke's Gospel, the conflict between Jesus and the Pharisees takes center stage. To appreciate Luke's prescriptions for spiritual health, we must understand the fundamental differences in the two views of religion represented by this conflict. The conflict and the contrast has persisted even into our own age. While we will return to additional religious comparisons in the last chapter, note for the present that the Pharisees and scribes saw the good life as one characterized by righteous living in accordance with religious rules. These were as clear and venerable as the "shalt nots" of the Ten Commandments. To make these rules for spiritually healthy living more precise (for implementation and enforcement), the Pharisees and scribes developed an incredibly extensive and elaborate system of specific laws for the Jewish people. Their work continued a long tradition of Jewish law-making, as consolidated in such Old Testament books as Leviticus and Deuteronomy.

Jesus challenged this rule-making tradition in theory and in practice. He argued that the Pharisees and scribes had missed the entire point of God's law. The healthy spiritual life consisted not in separation from sinners and slavish obedience to legal regulations but in practicing the law of love. The Holy Spirit is not a commodity to be hoarded by the righteous but to be shared with those most in need. Was healing work on the Sabbath a violation of God's law? Yes, said the Pharisees because this is *work* on the Sabbath. The commandment requires the Sabbath to be kept "holy"—i.e., separate—and to honor God's rest. Healing is a physician's work. No, said Jesus because this is *healing* on the Sabbath and the healing of broken, "dis-spirited" humans is God's desire.

This difference in perspective is evident in Luke's story of the healing of a man with a withered right arm. Luke observes: "The scribes and the Pharisees watched to see whether he [Jesus] would cure on the sabbath so that they might find an accusation against him"(6:7). Jesus asked the question, "Is it lawful to do good or do harm on the sabbath, to save life or to destroy it?" (6:9). Then he commanded the man to stretch out his arm: "He did so, and his hand was restored" (6:10). This act of healing on the Sabbath made the scribes and Pharisees furious. For them health was far less important than following their interpretation of the law—a law they could trace all the way back to Moses.

An interesting sidelight to this story is that Luke is the only Gospel writer to specify that the man's *right* arm was afflicted. That may reflect the doctor's concern for detail. But an apocryphal gospel says that the man was a stone mason who earned his living by hand, most likely his right hand. Here was a man who wanted to work, who was willing to try an improbable cure, and who came to Jesus with both hope and confidence. His remarkable healing was to be an object lesson for the orthodox religious leaders and also for the disciples, who were, in a sense, spiritual physicians in training.

After healing the man with a withered right arm, Luke tells us that Jesus "went to the mountains to pray; and he spent the night in prayer to God" (6:12). The next day, when he came down from the mountain with his disciples, he was met by "a great multitude of people . . . . And all in the crowd were trying to touch him, for power came out from him and healed all of them" (6:17-19).

By prayer Jesus took in the power of the Holy Spirit; through touch the power went out as a vital force to the afflicted; from example the disciples were to learn how to heal those in need—an act of love that distributed God's *pneuma* for a healthy humankind. Doing good and saving life are to replace "not working" as the Christian law of the Sabbath. This new religion was based not on prohibitions but on positive actions.

Immediately following these examples of healing and "medical discipleship," Luke presents the "Sermon on the Plain" (Luke's version of Matthew's "Sermon on the Mount"), in which Jesus outlined the blessings and rewards for those who *now* are needy, hungry, weeping, and suffering. Jesus also enumerated the woes that await those who *now* are rich, well-fed, laughing, and respected. The difference will be determined by the law of love. Those who can love even their enemies will find service in doing good and rich reward in heaven. Who will do good? Jesus taught his disciples that "a good person out of the good treasure of the heart produces good . . . for it is out of the abundance of the heart that the mouth speaks" (6:45). The Holy Spirit works from the inside out, empowering good people to do good works for God's kingdom, a kingdom where spiritual health is the norm. The disciples were commanded both to hear and act if they were to be Christ's physicians in the world.

Luke presses this line of reasoning even further. If Jesus can cure diseases and if blessings are to come to those in need through disciples who do good works and practice the law of love, what limits exist for the healing power of the Holy Spirit? To address this question Luke recounts an incident in Capernaum where a centurion was worried about a servant who was "ill and close to death" (7:2).

The centurion, an officer in the Roman army, was probably a Gentile and a person of some stature. Jews and Romans avoided each other most of the time, but this centurion had built a Jewish synagogue. Here was a man who had compassion for his slave, friendship with Jews, and a generous spirit—unusual indeed for a Roman soldier. Luke also points out that the centurion was a humble person who did not presume to approach Jesus in person, but sent a servant. Jesus admired this man for his attitude and his behavior. He turned to the crowd and declared, "I tell you, not even in Israel have I found such faith" (7:9). When the centurion's messengers returned to the house, they found the slave "in good health" (7:10).

But a patient "close to death" is not the ultimate test of Jesus' ability to heal physical affliction. In the next case chronicled by Luke, Jesus went to the town of Nain where he and his followers encountered a funeral in process. The dead man was the only son of his mother, a widow. Luke says when Jesus saw her, "he had compassion for her." He put his hand on the casket and said, "young man, I say to you, rise!" (7:13-14). The dead man sat up and began to speak. The reaction of the crowd is significant. Luke says, "Fear seized all of them; and they glorified God" (7:16).

This good news spread far and wide. Messengers came from John the Baptist, who wanted to know for certain if Jesus was the promised messiah. Luke reports that Jesus first responded with action and then with words:

> There and then he cured many sufferers from diseases, plagues, and evil spirits; and on many blind people he bestowed sight. Then he gave them his answer: "Go," he said, "and tell John what you have seen and heard: how the blind recover their sight, the lame walk, the lepers are made clean, the deaf hear, the dead are raised to life, the poor are hearing the good news—and happy is the man who does not find me a stumbling block" (7:21-23, NEB).

Luke's summary here makes it clear that Jesus was the master physician able to heal all of man's physical ills. There *are* no limits to the healing power of the Holy Spirit. But he also makes it clear that the Holy Spirit requires prayer and love by the physician and faith and humility from the patient.

Among these "many sufferers" with a variety of physical ailments was a child of twelve who was dying. This child was the only daughter of Jairus, a prominent Jew and president of the synagogue, who threw himself at Jesus' feet and begged him to come to his house to cure the child (8:41-42). Before Jesus could get away from the crowd, a messenger arrived with the sad news that the girl had died. Jesus came to the house and—accompanied by Peter, John, James, and the parents—went into the place where much weeping was going on. Luke reports that Jesus said, "Do not weep; for she is not dead but sleeping." Everyone laughed at him because they knew she was dead. Jesus then "took her by the hand and called out 'Child, get up!' Her spirit returned, and she got up at once. Then he directed them to give her something to eat" (8:49-56).

When the announcement first came that the child had died, Jesus responded: "Do not fear. Only believe, and she will be saved" (8:50). We should note that this healing followed the familiar incident where the disciples and Jesus were sinking in a storm as they crossed the Sea of Galilee in a small fishing boat. While the disciples displayed great panic, Jesus was fast asleep. They roused him and Jesus "rebuked the wind and the raging waves." The storm subsided and all was calm. Jesus then scolded the disciples: " Where is your faith?" he asked. In fear and astonishment they said to one another, "Who then is this, that he commands even the winds and the water, and they obey him? " (8:22-25). For Jairus, for the disciples, and for Jesus and his friends, the root problem is fear and the root cure is faith.

At the very time the messenger came from Jairus' house with the news that the young girl had died, Jesus was healing diseases of those who crowded around him. Among those was a frightened but brave woman who had been bleeding for twelve years. No one had been able to cure her, Luke observes, until she worked her way through the crowd and came close enough to touch the hem of Jesus' clothes. Jesus wondered who touched him "for I noticed that power had gone out from me" (8:46). The trembling woman came and fell at his feet, explaining to the people that this touch had provided an immediate cure. He said to her, "Daughter, your faith has made you well; go in peace" (8:48).

A twelve-year old girl and a woman with a twelve-year long hemorrhage: both given new life by the power of faith over fear. If only the disciples had such faith! We will return to the fear/faith dynamic in the next chapter.

Following these remarkable cases of healing, Luke says Jesus "called the twelve together and gave them power and authority to overcome all demons and to cure diseases, and he sent them out to proclaim the kingdom of God and to heal" (9:1-2). And the disciples then began their medical missionary work, for they "went through the villages, bringing the good news and curing diseases everywhere" (9:6). Of course, the ultimate test of the power of the Holy Spirit was in the resurrection of one who was dead and buried in a secure tomb: Christ himself.

These representative cases of physical ailments demonstrate Luke's unique perspective on the gospel of Jesus. As he sees it, Jesus is the master physician empowered by the Holy Spirit to cure every imaginable affliction of men and women, and dedicated to training up disciples who could do the same. Luke makes it known that patients—along with their friends and parents—have to bring something to the healing work of the physician. The famous latter-day physician William Osler had it right: when it comes to regaining health, the kind of patient may be more important than the kind of disease.

DR. LUKE'S PRESCRIPTIONS FOR PHYSICAL HEALTH

"We are small souls bearing up corpses."
—Epictetus

In our present day, medicine seems primarily concerned with those scientific and technological approaches that promise to fix the breakdowns of the body. Dr. Patrick Quillin notes that "America spends over $1 trillion each year on what we euphemistically call 'health care,' which is more 'disease maintenance' than anything else." He outlines some depressing health statistics:

- 58 million Americans have high blood pressure
- Half of us die from heart disease and one fourth from cancer; both diseases were relatively unknown in Abraham's time
- 24 million have insomnia
- 50 million have regular headaches

- 55 billion aspirin are consumed yearly
- 9 million are alcoholics
- 40 percent are overweight
- 40 million have mental illness
- 9.6 million older adults each year suffer drug-induced side effects, including 659,000 hospitalizations and 163,000 with memory loss *

As we begin the new millennium, more current statistics point to continuing concern in the area of health for the American population. For example, by 2000 statistics indicate that 59.7 million Americans have some form of cardiovascular disease, that 550,000 Americans will die of cancer, that 56 percent of American adults report symptoms of insomnia, that the number of alcoholics exceeds 14 million, that 43.1 percent of Americans are judged as "obese," and that more than 52,000 deaths are caused by illegal drugs. Of course, modern medicine has been a tremendous source of progress in the treatment of physical problems. Lasers, MRI's, drugs, sophisticated surgery—all have contributed to the relief of pain and suffering for contemporary society.

Dr. Luke's approach to physical health has a different emphasis. Because he believes health to be dependent on the Holy Spirit and the attitude of the patient, his prescriptions sound strange to the modern ear so accustomed to the scientific and technological approaches of our age. His perspective requires us to think about health as a spiritual matter, not merely "disease maintenance," and his prescriptions deal with our attitudes as well as our actions. Here are a few prescriptions:

R_x 1.
Understand Your Health as a Matter of Wholeness

As we have noted, the Greek word for health meant "whole," and Luke saw the health problems of his day as a matter of fractured and incomplete souls. His view of the

* *Healing Secrets from the Bible*, (Canton, Ohio, The Leader Company, 1995), p. 8.

body reflected the medicine of his day. A person was ill when the elements were out of balance and, especially, when the Holy Spirit and spirituality were in insufficient supply. Sin does cause sickness, in a way, because the sinner is an incomplete person separated from God. But God can and will supply the missing connection by his "vital force," the Holy Spirit, who will work within us to the extent we yield our lives to Jesus Christ, our Lord and Savior.

As Luke understood it, the greatest suffering is not from microscopic viruses or biochemical disorders but from a lack of unity in the soul itself. God wants people to be whole and well. For Luke that is the essence of the gospel message. And God's power is available for the patient who seeks it. All healing is an inside out process. All healing requires the active participation of the patient. All healing is a movement toward the restoration of the integrated self. Call on God's healing Holy Spirit to combat disease, dysfunction, and a dis-spirited body—and to restore wholeness.

R_x 2.
Watch What Goes in Your Mouth—
and What Comes Out

John the Baptist exemplified the "what goes in your mouth" aspect of the prescription. Recall that the angel declared even before John was born that he would "never touch wine or strong drink." With nine million alcoholics in the United States (perhaps explaining, in part, the consumption of 55 billion aspirin yearly!), such dietary discipline could serve our society well. But John's diet reflects other disciplines that contribute to a healthy life style. Given that our nation has some of the highest rates of any country for cancer, heart disease, and diabetes, a diet rich in fruits, vegetables, and grain is highly desirable for the health-conscious individual. That was the kind of food John the Baptist *did* put in his mouth.

The other side of this prescription—"what comes out" of your mouth—is one exemplified by Jesus. Concerned because the Pharisees used their strict dietary standards (outlined in Leviticus) as a defense of self-righteousness, he reminded them on many occasions that what comes out of one's mouth says much about the health of the soul. As the Proverb puts it, "As a [man] thinketh in his heart, so *is* he" (Prov. 23:7, KJV). Hate and envy are as poisonous to the spirit as alcohol is to the body. Jesus recommends thoughts and words of love and forgiveness. A diet is a disciplined menu of healthy choices: Good health requires attention to what we *choose* to put in our mouth and what we release from it by words expressing attitudes. Choose both diets wisely.

R_x 3.
Access the Holy Spirit's Power Through Prayer

For Luke, the Holy Spirit is an active force for treating diseases and afflictions of the body. How does this healing force actually get from God to man? In his Gospel, Luke sees healing working through the touch of Jesus—a direct physical connection between doctor and patient. In our day, medicine is re-discovering the importance of touch in such simple acts as hugging. The laying on of hands continues to be practiced in some forms of "faith healing." But the power to heal, as Luke sees it, requires the physician to go to God, the source of all health, in prayer.

In many of the events of physical healing described by Luke, Jesus turns to prayer. This is almost always solitary prayer in "lonely places." Jesus often repudiated the formal and public prayer of the orthodox religion of his day. Such prayer, he said, was more for show than for real communion with God. Both doctors and patients can breathe in the Holy Spirit by prayer that is private, personal, and power-full. If you expect God's Holy Spirit to work healing miracles in your life, you must open yourself to receive his power through effective prayer. Pray for God's healing power to make you well.

R_x 4.
Get Well to Serve Others

Those who are sick have a natural tendency to let their illness promote preoccupation with self. Much of the gospel message in Luke is devoted to the importance of service and self-sacrifice as an antidote to this self-absorption. Jesus served as the exemplar for such a life of service. This is the essence of *agape*, love so service oriented that the practitioner is willing to lay down his or her life for others. Luke sees this service motivation as an integral aspect of the healing process.

Remember, for example, that Simon's mother-in-law, cured of a high fever, "got up at once and waited on them." This is neither an accident nor a trivial point in Luke's description of the healing. Luke suggests that those who still have work to do and service to render are better candidates for survival than are others. This point is well made by World War II prison camp survivor Viktor Frankl in his illuminating book *Man's Search for Meaning*. Jesus himself saw service to others so central to his mission that he incurred the wrath of the Pharisees for healing on the Sabbath. Serve others—even your enemies—and you will find power for the healing of your afflictions.

R_x 5.
Express Gratitude for Your Cures

In Luke's philosophy of health, the attitude of the patient is paramount. Spiritual health should result in growth of a person's spiritual nature. One of the most important spiritual virtues is gratitude, a virtue Augustine called the "mature emotion." Luke is attentive to the development and expression of gratitude in the people Jesus heals. Some express gratitude through service (see prescription #4). In twelve-step self-help groups—such as Alcoholics Anonymous—the gratitude of the cured must be expressed in help to others with the same affliction. But there are other forms of expression.

Remember the cured leper who was asked by Jesus to

make an offering as required by Moses "to certify the cure" (5:14). And the cured paralytic who went home "praising God." In a later incident, Jesus cured ten men with leprosy but only one turned back, "praising God with a loud voice." The one, a Samaritan, "prostrated himself at Jesus' feet and thanked him." Of the other nine Jesus asked, "where are they?" (17:12-19). Expressing gratitude is more than a courtesy, more than a responsibility. It is a condition of the healthy spirit that takes no good happening for granted. When good health is yours, praise God.

R_x 6.
Exercise the Virtues of Love and Forgiveness

For Luke, the strongest medicines for all man's ills are love and forgiveness. As many learned at the feet of Jesus, service and gratitude are essentials in the arsenal of sound health. Love and forgiveness—so enduring they will extend to one's greatest persecutors—are hallmarks of the healthy spirit. These elixirs of life are not only good for the soul but for the body as well.

They are not mere sentimental emotions; they are virtues in action. They require getting out and doing things. You can't be a couch potato and develop spiritual health. Jesus put it this way: "You must love your enemies *and do good* (italics mine)" (6:35, NEB). And again: "The one who hears and *does not act* (italics mine) is like a man who built a house on the ground without a foundation" (6:49).

Later, in the house of Simon the Pharisee, Jesus points to a woman who had wet Jesus' feet with tears, wiped them with her hair, kissed them, and anointed them with myrrh. The Pharisees did none of these things for Jesus. Jesus said of her, "I tell you, her many sins have been forgiven—for she loved much" (7:47, NIV). Those who show in their actions the practice of love and forgiveness will receive love and forgiveness in return. Exercise these muscles in every move you make. Tone up the Christian physique. Make practice of these virtues a daily routine.

****

These are only a sample of the many prescriptions for physical health to be found in the book of Luke. They reflect the perspective of a first-century physician who is convinced that the Holy Spirit is a healing force for the faithful believers of Jesus. As we saw in the incident where Jesus first calmed the storm (while the disciples panicked) and later healed the timorous woman with the hemorrhage, faith is powerful medicine for the many ailments of fear. Because the quest for health—wholeness—is one that calls for an integrated self and unified soul, Luke's prescriptions for physical, mental, moral, financial, and religious health are all part of one piece.

It is the work of the Holy Spirit to put broken people back together again. And now modern medicine is rediscovering the "wisdom of the body" and the "prescription of the inner healer." Fear paralyzes but faith frees us to love. And love expressed in service to others provides motivation for the living of healthy lives.

But health is more than the absence of physical disabilities. In the next chapter we examine Luke's perspective on another aspect of illness, one also affected by fear: mental and psychological dysfunction.

CHAPTER 3

MENTAL HEALTH

"...All healing is faith healing."
—Sidney Jourard

Luke's Gospel has much to say about mental health. Luke portrays Jesus as an insightful physician (or therapist) who can diagnose the causes of mental illness and effect extraordinary cures. In most instances described by Luke, the afflicted were possessed by demons. The local folk believed these evil spirits were visited on a victim because of sin and at the behest of Satan. But Jesus saw the deranged as suffering from insufficient faith, misguided priorities, and impoverished spirit. Their major problems, Jesus said, are caused by fear.

The mentally ill are generally isolated from others (by their behavior and by social restrictions) and separated from God. Luke sees them as sad, angry, lonely, despairing human beings in need of a touch, a look, an understanding nod, a word of forgiveness, and a word of hope. These were Christ's therapeutic tools as he restored peace and sanity to the mentally anguished he encountered. How did Jesus prepare himself to deal with demons?

Following his baptism by John in the Jordan River, after "the Holy Spirit descended upon him in bodily form like a dove" (3:21-22), Jesus confronted his first demon, Satan himself. Luke tells us that Jesus was "full of the Holy Spirit" (4:1) and thus able to ward off the temptations of this master of all demons. How could Jesus cure others of their demons if he could not triumph in his own personal contest with the "great deceiver"?

The temptations of Satan were designed to distort Jesus' values and to turn his mind to the evils of material possessions and unbridled power. Jesus resisted them all by quoting the authority of the Scriptures. After resisting Satan's ploys, a spiritually strong Jesus began his healing work in Nazareth in the synagogue and made public reference to the proverb "Doctor, cure yourself" (4:23)—as, in a way, he had. His strength against the normal devilish temptations of humankind had come from the Holy Spirit. He was ready, now, to give orders to the unclean spirits with power and authority (4:35-36).

As we have seen, Jesus exercised his authority over fevers, diseases, and physical afflictions. But he also dealt with the demons of mental illness. In most such cases, Jesus penetrated the protective barriers of disabled behavior to get at the heart of the problem, a pathological fear (or phobia) that created paralysis, stress, panic, and irrational behavior.

Examples of Mental Healing

Luke's argument is that the cure for fear, invariably, is faith. Recall that Jesus' disciples were put into a great panic when a squall came up and their boat began to sink on the Sea of Galilee. When they ran to wake a sleeping Jesus, he "rebuked the wind and the raging waves." The storm subsided and all was calm. "Where is your faith?" he asked (8:22-25). There are storms on seas; storms create fear; fear leads to panic and ineffective behavior. But faith calms; faith creates confidence, faith relaxes; faith leads to effective behavior. Luke's point seems to be that the disciples need to learn how to exercise power over the storms of life. That power, derived from the Holy Spirit, is released only by acts of faith.

As a practical application of this principle, Luke follows with a powerful example of mental healing. When the boat lands in the country of the Gerasenes, the very first encounter for Jesus and the disciples was with a man from the town who was possessed by devils. Luke moves from a lesson in calming an *external* storm to a lesson in calming an *internal* storm of epic proportions. Luke describes the man and the encounter:

> For a long time he had worn no clothes, and he did not live in a house, but in the tombs. When he saw Jesus, he fell down before him and shouted at the top of his voice, "What have you to do with me, Jesus, Son of the Most High God? I beg you, do not torment me" (8:27-28).

The "tormenting," Luke says, referred to the exorcising of the unclean spirit that Jesus had begun immediately upon meeting the deranged demoniac.

As Luke's story continues, he tells us that the man had been "seized" many times in the past, that he had been chained for self protection, that he had always broken loose, and was "driven by the demons into the wilds" (8:29). We also learn that this man was called "Legion" because so many devils had possessed him.

These demons begged Jesus "not to order them to go back into the Abyss" (8:31), but to let them inhabit a herd of nearby pigs feeding on the hill. As Luke describes the event, the demons came out of the man, went into the pigs, and the entire herd "rushed down the steep bank into the lake and was drowned" (8:33). When the people came out to see what had happened, they found the man sitting at Jesus' feet, clothed, and "in his right mind" (8:35). Were they impressed? Thankful? Delighted? According to Luke, not at all. When the spectators told the people how the demoniac had been cured, the entire population of the town asked him to leave "for they were seized with great fear" (8:37).

The cured madman begged to go with Jesus, but Jesus sent him away: "Return to your home," he said, "and declare how much God has done for you" (8:39). And the man did exactly as Jesus requested.

We do not know the exact nature of the man's affliction—for Luke the spiritual conflict is as important as the psychological behavior—although medical speculation ranges from epilepsy to schizophrenia. What is uppermost in Luke's mind is the power of Jesus to calm the internal storm raging within the life of a man. We should also observe the "great fear" that gripped the people when they saw the madman cured. In Luke the attitude toward Jesus is frequently one of faith or fear.

Luke describes another incident of healing, in which Jesus drove out a man's devil which was dumb. When the man began to speak, the astonished people asked about the source of Jesus' authority over devils. Some thought it was Satan's power at work, but Jesus responded, "Any kingdom divided against itself will be ruined, and a house divided against itself will fall." His point was that Satan would hardly attack his own demons and thereby weaken his spiritual kingdom. Jesus suggested it was more logical to conclude that "I drive out demons by the finger of God" (11:17-19, NIV). How well this fits Luke's argument that Jesus, having been baptized by the Holy Spirit and having fortified his spiritual strength by prayer to God, communicated this healing "vital force" to those who boldly come to him in search of wholeness.

Luke takes this argument a step further in the passage immediately following. Jesus switched the metaphor slightly from a "divided kingdom" to an "unguarded castle." He told the same on-lookers: "When a strong man, fully armed, guards his castle, his property is safe. But when one stronger than he attacks him and overpowers him, he takes away his armor in which he trusted and divides his plunder" (11:21-22).

With yet another subtle shift of metaphor, Jesus concluded his discourse on demon possession by asking the crowd to think of the vulnerability of the "empty house." He offered this analogy:

> "When an unclean spirit has gone out of a person, it wanders through waterless regions looking for a resting place, but not finding any, it says 'I will return to my house from which I came.' When it comes, it finds it

swept and put in order. Then it goes and brings seven other spirits more evil than itself, and they enter and live there; and the last state of that person is worse than the first" (11:24-26).

Then Luke records a final admonition to the crowd: Jesus said, "Your eye is the lamp of your body. If your eye is healthy, your whole body is full of light; but if it is not healthy, your body is full of darkness" (11:34). A divided kingdom, an unguarded castle, an empty house, a darkened mind: each susceptible to invasion by demons and each a metaphor for the divided or diminished self.

What are we to make of such examples of demon possession and their implications for mental health? How did Jesus cure those who are controlled by evil spirits? What prescriptions for psychological wholeness might follow from the metaphorical messages Jesus gave to those who witnessed his healing power?

Dr. Luke's Prescriptions for Mental Health

> "A merry heart doeth good
> like a medicine: but a broken
> spirit drieth the bones."
> Proverbs 17:22, KJV

In the first century, Luke and his medical colleagues confronted many of the neurotic and psychotic personality disorders found in mental health clinics and psychiatric offices today. In our time, mental aberrations are usually viewed as diseases—often rooted in a complex of hereditary, environmental, and biochemical causes—and treatable by such modern means as drug therapy and psychoanalysis. In Luke's time, mental and psychological problems were viewed as spiritual concerns—rooted in sin and Satan—and treatable by demon exorcism. Jesus was not the only healer who exorcised demons, but his success was "astounding" and "amazing." Then and now mental disorders have been traumatic and mysterious, disorienting individuals and disrupting families.

The National Institute of Mental Health reminds us that the decade of the 1990s has been declared by Congress and the President as the "Decade of the Brain." This is to recognize tremendous accomplishments by researchers and the medical profession in diagnosing, treating, and preventing mental and brain disorders. And yet, mental illness continues to be a major problem for contemporary American society:

- One in five adults will have, at some time in life, mental illness that will require treatment

- Approximately 1.8 million people annually are affected by a form of schizophrenia

- Mood disorders—depression, mania, bipolar disorder—affect about 11.6 million adults each year

- Anxiety disorders affect more than 18 million people annually (more than 10 percent of the population)

- Alcohol dependence affects about 13 million Americans, including three million children; another 12.5 million suffer from substance abuse

- Among young people under the age of 18, some 12 million suffer from hyperactivity, autism, or depression

- Among children, suicide is the third leading cause of death

- Among the elderly, about 5 percent of those once labeled "senile" have some form of mental illness

The magnitude of mental illness in America suggests there is work to be done.

Interestingly enough, some current research points to imbalances among neurotransmitters (the brain chemicals that carry messages between nerve cells) as a cause for depression, schizophrenia, and other mental disorders. Could this be the re-discovery of the imbalance of *pneuma* in the mental life of individuals? Perhaps first-century Greek physicians were closer to the mark than our scientific age might suppose.

From Dr. Luke we have a number of prescriptions that are aimed at better mental health and which have value for the modern person:

R_x 1.
Check Your Spiritual Senses

According to Luke, it is no accident that Jesus spent much of his ministry giving check-ups to people whose senses were malfunctioning. Luke knew that the Holy Spirit needed clear pathways into the human soul if the *pneuma* was to do its work for mental health. While healing the blind, deaf, and dumb appear on the surface to be mere physical healings, Luke keeps reminding us that the real sense problems are spiritual in nature. Why is a prophet not accepted in his own country (4:24)? Poor spiritual vision. Why, Jesus asks his disciples, do you "call me Lord, Lord, and do not do what I tell you?" (6:46). Poor spiritual hearing. Why do the disciples not know how to pray (11:1) or how to ask that they might receive (11:9)? Poor spiritual speech.

Mental illness often manifests itself in distorted perceptions of reality. Some paranoid personalities see enemies in every stranger. Some illnesses of delusion produce the voices of long gone relatives—or famous figures from history. The mentally depressed can hear no word of hope even from their most positive friends. In explaining the parable of the sower to his disciples, Jesus assured them: "To you it has been given to know the secrets of the kingdom of God; but to others I speak in parables, so that looking they may not perceive, and listening they may not understand"(8:10).

The Holy Spirit needs pathways to the mind. Keep yours in good working order by letting Jesus heal the pathways to your soul. Keep your heart and mind open to God's voice. Let the pure light and life of the Scriptures minister to you each day. And most of all, let God's love purify your soul as you grow in Christ Jesus. The more you allow Jesus into your life, the healthier your mind and soul will be.

R_x 2.
Admit Your Illness

Many people are either self-delusional or deliberately unresponsive to the call to spiritual health. The people Jesus cured invariably were those who knew their need (Jesus said, "how blest are you who are in need; the kingdom of God is yours"), and who sought his curing power. The demoniac, for example, declared that his name was "Legion" because he knew that he was in the control of a legion of demons. Facing spiritual problems (or any problems) directly and asking for help is almost always the first step toward curing human ills. The demoniac displayed great honesty and humility when he came to Jesus for a release from the demons that haunted his life.

Could these have been the demons of loneliness? Perhaps loneliness was the cause, rather than the result, of his illness. Recall that this demoniac did not even live in a house but in the tombs, an isolated place of despair and death. In *The Broken Heart*, Dr. James Lynch, a researcher at Johns Hopkins, concludes that loneliness is the psychological malady that is the major cause of death in America. Those who live alone, he says, have a premature death rate two to ten times higher than individuals who live with others.

In contrast to the demoniac, the Pharisees were so self-righteous they saw no need of the Holy Spirit; they could admit no spiritual illness; they thought they were in perfect spiritual health. In *There's a Lot More to Health than Not Being Sick*, Bruce Larson says, "it takes a lot of psychic energy to maintain this constant posture of rightness and eventually our bodies are going to pay the price for the stress that results" (p. 16). Psychological counseling only works when the patient lowers the defense mechanisms. Larson observes that "the very heart of sin is to play at innocence.... If I own my mistakes and my sins and can say that I and no one else is responsible for them, then I can be forgiven" (p. 20). Jesus put it this way: "The heavenly Father [will] give the Holy Spirit to those who ask him!" (11:13). Know your need, admit your weakness, ask for help.

R_x 3.
Seek a Cure Boldly but Humbly

Psychological growth and the journey to spiritual maturity require boldness. In Luke, those who show courage find cures for their maladies. That was true for the woman with a hemorrhage and the paralytic. It was also true for the naked and homeless demoniac. Psychiatrist Scott Peck, in *Further Along the Road Less Traveled: The Unending Journey Toward Spiritual Growth*, says:

> We can only go forward through the desert of life, making our way painfully over parched and barren ground into increasingly deeper levels of consciousness...but the journey is hard and consciousness often painful. And so most people stop their journey as quickly as they can. They find what looks like a safe place and burrow into the sand, and stay there rather than go forward through the painful desert, which is filled with cactuses and thorns and sharp rocks (p. 19).

Mental illness is one way to "burrow into the sand" of life and avoid the "sharp rocks" of suffering, pain, rejection, and despair. This is what Peck calls "neurotic suffering," an unconstructive way to deal with anxiety and guilt that can be remedied only by courage to go ahead in spite of the pain.

In his own wilderness desert, Jesus confronted Satan courageously and resisted all of his wily and seductive temptations. Be bold, Jesus told the disciples: "Ask and it will be given to you; seek and you will find; knock and the door will be opened to you" (11:9, NIV). He might have added: If opportunity doesn't knock, build a door. There are many professional agencies and individuals who can provide counsel, support, and services for those in the grip of fear, distress, and isolation. The afflicted person, however, must be willing to take the first step. Be bold in seeking mental health.

But also be humble. It was pride that kept the Pharisees from spiritual growth. In one graphic contrast, Luke describes the prayer of the Pharisee who confessed his goodness: "God, I thank you that I am not like other people: thieves, rogues, adulterers, or even like this tax collector." Next to him was a tax collector, a sinner who prayed: "God, be merciful to me, a sinner!" Jesus said it was the tax collector who went home forgiven of his sins, "for all who exalt themselves will be humbled, but all who humble themselves will be exalted" (18:10-14). Go through the desert, toward God, with the right combination of bold humility. Take the path to true mental health.

R_x 4.
Beware the Temptations That Distort Reality

One of the major symptoms of mental illness—in several of its manifestations—is the patient's skewed view of himself and the world. For example, addicts often deny the actuality of their addiction. Or they blame stress, heredity, their spouses—or anyone else they can think of—for their choices, dependencies, and behavior. Addictions, whether to alcohol or gambling or drugs or food, are often merely the logical extremes of human appetite yielded to in temptation. How easy it is to see ourselves as victims who have no responsibility and no choice in the lives we lead.

In *Further Along the Road Less Traveled*, Scott Peck makes the intriguing argument that

> One way of looking at addictions is to see them as forms of idolatry. For the alcoholic the bottle becomes an idol.... People who become slaves to alcohol and other drugs are people who want, who yearn, to go back to Eden—who want to reach Paradise, reach heaven, reach home—more

than most.... [But] the only way to reach home is the hard way (pp. 136-137).

He adds that Carl Jung, the great psychiatrist who saw "Holy Scripture [as]...utterances of the soul,"* observed it was no accident that we call alcoholic drinks "spirits." Alcoholism is perhaps a "spiritual disorder."

In similar ways, those who are psychotic (split from reality) and neurotic (obsessed by reality) do not have a clear focus on what is real and what is important. No wonder they are "separated" from the most important reality of life: the one true living God. Their souls are "divided houses" where demons take up residence and undermine mental health.

Mentally and psychologically healthy people have a clear view of God's nature and their own. They know what is theirs and what is God's. They know what God wants from them and what they need from him. Their values and priorities are aligned with the path of spiritual growth. They know how to establish healthy relationships with others and with the material world. They are at peace with God, their fellow humans, and themselves. Now, this may be the very point of the encounter Jesus had with Satan in the wilderness. Note that Satan attempted to distort Jesus' values to pit him against God, humanity, and the physical world. Jesus would have none of it: "Worship the Lord your God, and serve only him" (4:8). We should do likewise. The reward will be peace of mind and oneness with God. Resist the temptations that keep you from seeing and serving God.

R_x 5.
Guard the Fortress of the Mind
Prevention is a key element in maintaining mental health. As Jesus put it, "when a strong man, fully armed, guards his castle, his property is safe" (11:21). Whether we look at the

---

* For an insightful analysis of Jung's views on the relation of psychology and religion, see Wayne G. Rollins, *Jung and the Bible*, John Knox Press: Atlanta, GA, 1983.

mind as a kingdom (that should not be divided) or a castle (that should not be unguarded) or a house (which should not be left empty), it is clear that Jesus and Luke knew the importance of prevention in the achievement of mental health. Prevention of what? For Luke it was probably the demons that invade any unprotected self. In our day, prevention might include protection against stress, foreign addictive substances, destructive relationships, faulty rationalization and other defense mechanisms, television violence, and faulty parenting.

What can you do to protect yourself and your children from the assault on mental and psychological wellness? Here are but a few preventive measures any good guardian of the mind might take:

- *Work on providing a safe and secure family environment.* Research suggests that insecure and unhappy infants have trouble with trust of others in later life. Abused children often fail as parents.

- *Learn the symptoms of mental illness.* This includes recognizing problems in self-concept development (low self-esteem has a powerful role in depression and eating disorders), physiological behaviors associated with psychotic and neurotic disorders, and sociological behaviors signaling relationship difficulties.

- *Develop strategies that reduce stress.* Such strategies include proper diet, exercise, relaxation, and physical check-ups. Find ways to enjoy yourself: live, love, learn, and leave a legacy (as Stephen Covey recommends). Laughter is the best medicine (as *Reader's Digest* reminds us). Give time to serve the welfare of others.

- *Spend time in reflection, meditation, Bible study, and prayer.* These spiritual activities can keep you in balance and protect you from the assaults of the world on your spiritual nature.

Take preventive measures to guard your house from the

mental conflicts that divide; protect the defenseless self which is easy prey for evil spirits.

R_x 6.
Replace Fear with Faith

Time and again, Jesus provided this spiritual prescription for those who would overcome the maladies of mind that depress, distort, distract, and deprive people of true health. Luke records event after event where the cure for fear is faith. Indeed, the phrases "do not be afraid" or "fear not" appear frequently in Luke's narrative to provide reassurance:

- For Zechariah and Mary on the miraculous births of John and Jesus (1:13, 30)

- For the shepherds keeping watch over their sheep (2:10)

- For the disciples as they were sinking on the Sea of Galilee (8:25)

- For the president of the synagogue whose daughter had died (8:50)

It is fear that blocks the healing power of the Holy Spirit, but faith lets the Holy Spirit work a miracle for physical and mental health.

What was the "great fear" that gripped the "normal" people in the Gerasenes when the madman was cured by Jesus? Perhaps they feared their loss of income when a valuable herd of pigs was drowned; perhaps they feared a change in their daily routines when a madman was made whole again. How accepting are we of the mentally disturbed? How willing to make room for them in our neighborhoods? Our fears, too, are legion.

Luke's "good news" is that faith can replace fear as a dynamic in spiritual wellness. The faith of a mustard seed can move mountains. Luke's claim is more modest: "The apostles said to the Lord, 'Increase our faith!' The Lord replied, 'If you had faith the size of a mustard seed, you could say to this mulberry tree, "Be uprooted up and planted in the sea," and it would obey you'" (17:5-6). What power there is in faith!

In *Love, Medicine and Miracles*, Dr. Bernie Siegel notes that "about one-fourth to one-third of patients will show improvement if they merely *believe* they are taking an effective medicine..." (p. 35). He adds that "a patient's hope and trust lead to a 'letting go' that counteracts stress and is often the key to getting well" (p. 35); and "the body can utilize any form of energy for healing...as long as the patient believes in it" (p. 129). Sidney Jourard's remarkable book *The Transparent Self* suggests that physicians and mental health workers "begin seriously to study 'spirit' as a natural phenomenon" because "all healing is faith healing... [and] faith triggers off an increase in spirit..." (p. 83). Faith in the Holy Spirit, says Luke, frees us from fear and empowers us to be children of God. Take this good medicine for spiritual health.

****

In her contemporary work as Director of the Mind/Body Clinic at the Harvard Medical School, Dr. Joan Borysenko has dealt with the relationship between physical and mental health. In *Minding the Body, Mending the Mind* she makes this observation:

> We are already perfect—our essential core is peaceful and whole. The work of healing is in peeling away the barriers of fear and past conditioning that keep us unaware of our true nature of wholeness and love (p. 4).

That "perfection," Luke might contend, is only possible when faith is perfect and fear is abolished from the human soul. Luke shows us the perfect example of "wholeness and love" in the life of Jesus. The Holy Spirit, Luke argues, can work such miracles of healing for all manner of disease and affliction, mental as well as physical. One who wants a healthy soul must also attend to another dimension of life: the moral.

CHAPTER 4

MORAL HEALTH

"Be master of your will and a slave to your conscience."
—Lieb Lazerow

Luke's Gospel message of spiritual health does not neglect the moral realm. If health is wholeness, then we should live in the light of the whole truth. Moral truth should lead to virtuous living in accordance with the highest principles of honesty, and culminate in behavior totally consistent with spiritual values. That is to say, what we understand, believe, and do should be of a piece, a seamless web of knowledge, faith, and action. Such congruence is at the heart of the integrated life: a life without moral conflicts or ambiguities or deceptions. In a word, a life of *integrity*. What does Dr. Luke diagnose as moral illness? What antidotes did Jesus provide? How do we live a life of moral wellness? What is the path to integrity?

As we have already seen, Luke begins his Gospel account (to give Theophilus "authentic knowledge" in a "connected narrative") with the birth stories of John the Baptist and Jesus, each infant filled with the Holy Spirit. Each was a moral exemplar but in different ways. John exemplified morality by self-discipline and abstemious behavior; Jesus exemplified morality by self-sacrifice and bold truth-telling. John developed the strength of his character away from crowds in the isolated nature of the wilderness. Jesus developed the depth of his love in the communal centers of the temple and the marketplace.

Luke portrays John's moral preaching as a kind of preparation for Jesus' higher moral principles. Quoting Isaiah, Luke calls John "The voice of one crying in the wilderness: 'Prepare the way of the Lord, make his paths straight'" (3:4-5). Preaching the principle of repentance, John chastises the crowds as a "brood of vipers" and criticizes them for failing "to bear good fruit." Repent, he says, because your unethical behavior condemns you to the fire.

His admonitions for ethical living are given in response to a question from the crowd:

> "Whoever has two coats must share with anyone who has none; and whoever has food must do likewise." Even tax collectors came to be baptized, and they asked him, "Teacher, what should we do?" He said to them, "Collect no more than the amount prescribed for you." Soldiers also asked him, "And we, what should we do?" He said to them, "Do not extort money from anyone by threats and false accusation, and be satisfied with your wages" (3:10-14).

The only other point Luke makes about John's moral crusade is that when John rebuked the powerful Prince Herod for his incestuous and illicit affair with his brother's wife Herodias, Herod threw John in prison. John's moral courage cost him his life (3:19-20).

Luke's greater interest, of course, is the moral life and teaching of Jesus. He describes the growth of Jesus and the nurturing of his noble character. How did Jesus grow so strong and wise?

First, Luke assures us, Jesus was from conception forward inspired by and guided by the Holy Spirit. His integrity was guaranteed by Gabriel, nourished by a loving Mary, endorsed by visiting shepherds, and confirmed in his first days of infancy by the "rite of purification" in accordance with the Law of Moses.

Second, Luke tells us, Jesus received support from faithful leaders of the Jewish faith: Simeon, who was "righteous and devout" (2:25) and Anna, "of a great age" who "never left the temple but worshiped there with fasting and prayer night and day" (2:36-38). Both gave praise and thanks to God for this special child.

Third, Luke tells us, Jesus learned from his teachers. In one famous incident during Passover, Jesus was lost when his parents thought he was with relatives. They returned to the Holy City three days later to find him "in the temple, sitting among the teachers, listening to them and asking them questions. And all who heard him were amazed at his understanding and his answers" (2:41-51).

Luke concludes this description of Jesus' early development by simply observing: "And Jesus grew in wisdom and stature, and in favor with God and men" (2:52, NIV).

Jesus' Teachings on Moral Health

According to Luke, at the beginning of his work teaching the disciples, Jesus presented them with the new moral standard that should guide them. In the Sermon on the Plain (6:20-49), he reminded them that heaven and earth judge goodness and dispense rewards on quite different terms: the rich and happy on earth will be poor and weeping in the life to come. Those who lived by the new moral standards could expect pain and suffering in the world (witness John the Baptist) but "your reward is great in heaven" (6:23). He warned the disciples that they will be hated, insulted, and banned "on account of the Son of Man" (6:22), a messianic title he applied to himself.

Jesus then outlined his moral code of conduct for disciples in the world. Notice how his code paralleled John's principles of just behavior, but went much further in the requirement for love and forgiveness:

"Love your enemies, do good to those who hate you, bless those who curse you, pray for those who abuse you. If anyone strikes you on the cheek, offer the other also; and from anyone who takes away your coat do not withhold even your shirt. Give to everyone who begs from you; and if anyone takes away your goods, do not ask for them again. Do to others as you would have them do to you. . . . Be merciful, just as your Father is merciful" (6:27-36).

There is more: do not judge others, do not condemn, do give. Do these things, Jesus taught, and you will have a rich reward, "for the measure you give will be the measure you get back" (6:38).

This set of moral precepts was to guide his students, the disciples, as they ministered to the spiritual health of the world. Moral sins were to be remedied by the strong spiritual medicine of love, repentance, and forgiveness. Jesus knew this was harder in practice than in theory. Will the disciples really learn the principles of this powerful new ethic? He had given them his personal example and his moral principles. Jesus then found another way to help the disciples not only *hear* the word but to *act* on it. Could the disciples grasp the high cost of Jesus' ethic? To be a disciple, Jesus said, meant to "deny themselves and take up their cross daily and follow me" (9:23) How did Jesus teach this ethic of total service? By object lessons embodied in parables.

While Jesus presented a strong moral character—and lived it out by clear teaching, bold preaching, and authoritative healing—he found his integrity challenged by the religious leaders of his day. As Luke interprets it, this challenge offered an instructional opportunity for the disciples. The scribes and Pharisees provide the major value conflict in Jesus' ministry: religion based on rules versus religion based on love. Jesus used this conflict as an object lesson in morality for the pious leaders and the slow-learner disciples. This object lesson taught them new ways to look at questions of good and bad, true and false, right and wrong. In the process, Jesus turned prevailing concepts of morality upside down.

This opportunity came in the form of a test question put to Jesus by a scribe, a lawyer of religious law. His response came in the form of a parable, one of his best known parables and one which appears only in Luke's Gospel. It is a morality play that we know as the Parable of the Good Samaritan.

Parables

Jesus frequently used parables as a way to make abstract principles concrete. The word *parable* etymologically means "thrown down alongside," that is, a comparison. Parables are highly metaphorical illustrations, and Jesus drew his illustrations from nature, common life, and familiar incidents. It is possible, maybe even likely, that the events in the Parable of the Good Samaritan actually happened. But Jesus told parables to make specific comparisons and significant points: in this case a point about moral behavior consistent with the ethical principles he has just outlined for the disciples.

Those who listened to Jesus' parables—frequently scribes and Pharisees, crowds of on-lookers, and disciples—were drawn to these vivid stories and intriguing metaphors, but they didn't always understand them. That may be because such "word pictures" were compelling but complex comparisons.

In *Teaching For Faith*, Richard Osmer argues that, though parables appear to be a device by which Jesus clarified complex theological concepts by way of concrete illustrations, a parable actually "flies in the face of everything that makes sense in our normal way of looking at things." Osmer explains:

> A parable is a brief story, based on everyday life, that brings about a sudden reversal of the expectations of its hearers, opening them up to a new way of seeing God and the world in relation to God. Far from being a simplified teaching illustration, a parable attempts to make strange what is normally taken for granted. It does this by a sudden, unexpected reversal of the audience's expectations (p. 152).

That a Samaritan—the *least* moral person in the common view of Jewish society—should turn out to be the most responsible "neighbor" would certainly arrest the attention of Jesus' audience and perplex all who were listening. Indeed, the very idea of a "good Samaritan" would shock the Jewish listeners to the core of their moral expectations.

Parables have been described as earthly stories with heavenly meanings, as signposts to the kingdom of heaven, and as riddles that tease the mind into active thought. Although Jesus explained a few of his parables, he left the meaning of the Parable of the Good Samaritan to the moral judgment of the scribe. What began as an abstract theological question Jesus turned into a concrete example of first aid; when asked about eternal life, Jesus told a story about room and board at a local hotel. Jesus turned the debate about heaven into an issue of health for body *and* soul. Let us take a closer look at this well-known parable of ethical behavior.

The Good Samaritan

This moral fable appears to be a simple story designed to answer a question raised by the scribe, who was trying to test Jesus on his knowledge of Moses' Law. Here Jesus answered questions with questions: The scribe asked, "What must I do to inherit eternal life?" Jesus answered, "What is written in the law?" The scribe replied, "You shall love the Lord your God with all your heart, and with all your soul, and with all your strength, and with all your mind; and your neighbor as yourself." Jesus said, "You have given the right answer; do this, and you will live" (10:25-28).

But the scribe "wanted to justify himself" and so asked another question to Jesus: "And who is my neighbor?" Jesus responded with a story followed by yet another question. In the familiar story, a man traveling from Jerusalem to Jericho, a dangerous road for any traveler, was attacked by robbers who left him half dead. A priest and a Levite—two (supposedly) moral leaders—passed him by, but a Samaritan was moved to pity and took care of the man. He bandaged his wounds, bathing them with oil and wine (a common medical practice Luke would know well), took him to an inn, looked after him, paid the innkeeper two silver pieces to keep an eye on the recovering victim, and promised to pay more if needed on his way back.

The question Jesus put to the scribe was, "Which of these three, do you think, was a neighbor to the man who fell into the hands of the robbers?" The scribe replied, "The one who showed him mercy." Jesus said, "Go and do likewise" (10:36-37). Now, in many ways the meaning of the parable is obvious. But it will be useful for our purposes to elaborate, remembering that parables are never simple, always tease the mind into active thought, and challenge prevailing assumptions and logic.

First, a note about the *setting*. The road down from Jerusalem to Jericho is precipitous: it descends 3,600 feet in about twenty miles by way of a twisting, rocky road ideal for marauding bandits. They could hide behind boulders and spring upon unsuspecting travelers going down from the "Holy City" of Jerusalem to a great "City of Commerce," Jericho. Attacks were so frequent on this highway that it still had the name "The Bloody Way" in the fifth century A.D., and even in the nineteenth century travelers bribed local leaders to protect themselves from the Bedouin. The road downward from religion to commerce is dangerous indeed.

Second, a note about the *characters*. We do not know who the robbers were; we only know they constituted risks along the road. The priest and the Levite (a minor priest) were religious leaders, highly-respected Jews who knew the Law of Moses and were considered the most moral of men. They were likely coming from, or going to, Jerusalem where they performed religious duties in the temple of the Holy City. Samaritans were considered, at best, "half-Jews," and true Jews despised them. Samaritans traced their origins to Jews of the Northern Kingdom who had intermarried with the hated Assyrian invaders, who had conquered Israel and destroyed Samaria in 722 B.C. Samaritans were in such disgrace that they were not permitted to help rebuild the temple in Jerusalem when Ezra and Nehemiah brought the Judean Jews back from exile in Babylon (c. 535 B.C.). Considered renegades and law breakers (they rejected all of the Old Testament except for the Pentateuch), they were certainly not friends or "neighbors" of the Jews. And the man who was robbed and beaten? We have no clue to his identity, but we can at least infer that he was either brave or foolish to travel such a risky road alone.

Third, a note about the *plot*. The unwary and unwise traveler was set upon by robbers, stripped, and left to die. The priest and the Levite, both law-abiding Jews, walked by on the other side. Why? Because the Law of Moses (Numbers 19:11) said anyone who touched a dead body was unclean for seven days. If these two religious leaders were on their way to the temple in Jerusalem, they might be prohibited from the high point of their lives: participating in religious ceremonies in the Holy City. Besides, if the man was not dead, he might well be a decoy, a common ploy by robbers to lure unsuspecting passers-by to their lair.

Finally, a note about the *theme*. There are many messages of value in this striking parable, but the one that is most telling reveals the essence of Christian virtue. Morality is never merely a matter of following the law. The priest and the Levite demonstrated that all too well. Nor is morality merely a virtuous but passive sentiment, such as pity. The purpose of moral law is found in action, an ethic of love manifested in helping and in healing. The question the lawyer turned back on himself was not "who is my neighbor?" but "who am I?" Am I a neighbor to anyone who needs me? For Jesus, this was the theme the lawyer needed to hear. The Samaritan was the most moral person in the parable. He alone was prepared to help because his love was not limited by law nor by a definition; it sought not its responsibilities but its opportunities. The priest and the Levite left their love in the temple. The Samaritan took his love on life's risky road—and put it to work. What a shocking insight into true morality! What a paradox for the legalists to contemplate!

The Pharisees, who considered themselves the most righteous and holy of all Jews, were characterized by Jesus as even
less moral than the priest and Levite. This becomes evident as
Luke's narrative continues to address questions of true
integrity and the ethics of love. Luke relates an incident at a
Pharisee's house when Jesus, an invited guest, was chastised
by his host for not washing before the meal. Jesus confronted
the Pharisee (and later the scribes) with a series of shocking
charges against their false standard of morality. The major
charge: hypocrisy.

When the Pharisee questioned Jesus' failure to wash in
accordance with the ritual cleansing required of "righteous"
Jews, he responded:

> "Now you Pharisees clean the outside of the cup and of
> the dish, but inside you are full of greed and wickedness.
> You fools! Did not the one who made the outside make
> the inside also?" (11:39-40).

Jesus followed this accusation with a series of "woe" state-
ments: "Woe to you Pharisees! For you tithe mint and rue and
herbs of all kinds, and neglect justice and the love of
God....Woe to you! For you are like unmarked
graves..."(11:42-44). And then he added: "Woe also to you
lawyers! For you load people with burdens hard to bear, and
you yourselves do not lift a finger to ease them" (11:46).

What are these strong accusations all about? Jesus bluntly
charged the Pharisees and scribes with focusing on the
appearance of morality—laws, rituals, external shows of
virtue—but being rotten at the core. They went through the
motions of virtue but their hearts were full of self righteousness and greed. Instead of helping others, lifting their load,
they attempted to horde the rewards of virtue for themselves.
Selfishness is never moral. For Jesus, the real paradox is "self-
righteous virtue." The self-righteous are never truly virtuous.

Jesus did indeed turn the prevailing notions of morality

upside down. Luke's accounts of Jesus' parables and sayings provide sound prescriptions for ethical behavior in all times.

DR. LUKE'S PRESCRIPTIONS
FOR MORAL HEALTH

"Be not simply good. Be good for something."
—Henry David Thoreau

Some 2,000 years after Jesus set forth his law of love and his high expectations for Christian values, we should have made some progress toward moral health. And yet, the United States today seems mired in moral imperfection of unprecedented proportions. Political leaders at the highest levels are assailed by scandal and charges of corruption. Our cities are described in the press as cesspools of degradation and crime. Families are under siege as social values and family unity are in disarray. Schools and churches seem no longer able to promote a common core of virtues once assumed as a given in American culture.

Consider the following contemporary conditions and statistics as indicators of our moral health, or lack thereof:

* Over one million teenagers become pregnant every year and forty percent of today's fourteen-year-old girls will become pregnant by the time they are nineteen

* The national illegitimacy rate is predicted to reach 50 percent within the next twelve to twenty years

* In 1962, fewer than four million Americans had ever experimented with illegal drugs; in 1996 the number was 80 million; in 1997 an estimated 2.1 million began smoking cigarettes daily with more than 3000 per day under the age of 18

* From 1990 to 1991 illegal drug abuse has cost America

more than $300 billion and 100,000 deaths (and at present the medical cost of drug abuse exceeds $20 billion per year); in 1998 an estimated 13.6 million were users of illegal drugs

- An estimated 525,000 attacks, shakedowns, and robberies occur in public high schools each month
- Each year nearly three million crimes are committed on or near school property and about 135,000 students carry guns to school daily
- At the beginning of the new millennium, trends are decidedly toward higher poverty rates and higher divorce rates, toward higher crime and illegal drug use rates
- In 1996 one automobile was stolen every twenty seconds in the United States

No, we cannot claim for ourselves or our nation anything like moral goodness. Dr. Luke's prescriptions can help:

R_x 1.
Live by a Clear Moral Code

As part of his teaching ministry, Jesus gave to his disciples a code of conduct that went even further than John the Baptist's in outlining principles to live by. Some of these principles he taught by personal example, some by direct pronouncement, and some by parables. Always these principles of right thought and action were governed by a unifying master principle: the law of love. Any pious Jew, certainly the Pharisees who kept the essential Mosaic Law written in phylacteries on their foreheads, knew this law: It contained the twin requirements: 1) Love God with all your heart, soul, and mind; 2) Love your neighbor as yourself. In all his moral teaching, Jesus attempted to show how this law should be translated into specific principles to guide specific behavior.

The essentials of Jesus' moral code were simple, direct, and clear. For him the challenge was always to *live* by the code, to put it into routine practice, to *do* the law of love in all of life's circumstances. These principles of love in action include the following:

- Love your enemies and pray for them—anyone can love friends.

- Return good for evil, turning the other cheek.

- Give to all who ask and all who need—they are all your neighbors.

- Never judge others, only forgive and serve them.

- Do not be hearers of the word only but doers of the word.

- Always put the welfare of others ahead of your own.

- Put God's approval ahead of man's, no matter the consequences.

- Be bold in speaking up for God against the world.

- Pray humbly before God, confessing your sin and asking for mercy.

- Put total child-like trust in the goodness of God.

There are more such principles of moral behavior, of course, but these will serve. Notice that each standard contains both an *attitude* and an *action*. Love is not merely an emotion, an abstract concept, a romanticized sentiment; it is for Dr. Luke strong medicine when it governs thought *and* deed. You must not only have a moral code: you must live by it.

R_x 2.
Practice Kindness

If you live by a clear moral code, you can find all of the principles you need in the book of Luke. The law of love has many applications, as we noted in the previous prescription for moral health, but kindness is a special application that requires more discussion. We live in an age when kindness seems to be a diminishing quality in human relationships. Incivility seems to be the norm and rudeness prevails far too often—on the highway, in the supermarket check-out line, on the playground, and in the workplace. Jesus was nothing if not kind. Yes, he was bold and he even displayed his anger on occasion, but he practiced a high level of civility and kindness. How did Jesus teach kindness?

First, by what he *said*: "bless those who curse you," "pray for those who treat you spitefully," "treat others as you would have them treat you." These are admonitions to be kind. The Parable of the Good Samaritan elevates acts of kindness to a new level of civility: true neighborliness. Remember, too, his teachings about friendship, hospitality, courtesy at dinner parties. The kindness of the disciples was to extend to forgiving others not seven times but seventy times seven, and loaves and fishes were to be shared in love with thousands: "give them something to eat yourselves." Be kind, said Jesus.

Second, by what he *did*. He showed kindness in his curing and compassion in his caring. "If anyone wishes to be a follower of mine, he must leave self behind," he said. And he did that even to his sacrificial death on the cross. He reached out to the ill and he took children in his arms. His look and his touch communicated his essential kindness to all who were in need: "Ask...search...knock, and the door will be opened" (11:9). That is heavenly kindness at its best.

Do you speak encouraging words to others? Are your tendencies toward forgiveness rather than revenge? Do you have a generous heart, a listening ear, and eyes that see needs? How do you measure up on the courtesy scale? Do you reach out to others and touch them with true compassion? If so, you are practicing kindness in what you say and do. A modern aphorism says, "no good deed goes unpunished." So? Great is your reward in heaven. Whatever the situation and whatever the consequences: Be kind.

R_x 3.
Practice Humility

Humility. What a difficult virtue to master! Benjamin Franklin, that exemplar of Enlightenment optimism, once set forth a bold program to arrive at moral perfection. As he described it in his *Autobiography*, he identified thirteen specific virtues and systematically chartered his progress in acquiring each virtue in turn: temperance, frugality, chastity, and so on. The final virtue was "humility." His goal was to conclude his mastery of morality by developing perfect humility. What irony! The trouble with self-made men is that they tend to worship their creator. Be humble, Jesus taught, not because you can achieve moral perfection but because you never can. Only God is perfectly good. The greatest sin of humans is pride, a false sense of one's own goodness.

Luke stresses the importance of humility throughout his Gospel as he prescribes his medicine for spiritual health. Jesus himself was born of common Jewish parents in the most humble of settings: a manger behind a crowded inn. He grew up in a carpenter's shop and never acquired any of the trappings of power or influence of the upper crust in his society. Satan could not tempt him with possessions and fame. He promised his disciples persecution and hardship in this world and required them to go into the world empty-handed: "Take nothing for your journey, no staff, nor bag, nor bread, nor money—not even an extra tunic" (9:3). And he died a common death, humbled by a mocking crown of thorns. From birth in a manger to death on a cross, Jesus' life exemplified perfect humility.

Recognize your need. Practice true humility. It is the perfect virtue. You can *never* master it. Be humble.

R_x 4.
Develop a Healthy Self-Discipline

Luke tells us that John the Baptist exemplified a Spirit-filled life of dedication to self-discipline, and he paid the ultimate price for his high ethical standards. He avoided wine and strong drink and ate a healthy diet by standards of our day as well as his own. His Nazirite discipline was reflected in values designed to promote good physical and moral health. He advocated a simple but demanding ethical code consistent with his religious beliefs: 1) share with those in need, 2) be honest in the workplace, 3) don't bully or coerce others, 4) be satisfied with your pay, 5) stay pure in your relations with others. One other value he lived (and died) by was this: stand up for these values no matter the consequence.

Luke discusses self-discipline and dedication to high ethical values in the lives of Jesus and the disciples, too. In the Sermon on the Plain Jesus tells the disciples that moral health is difficult but worth the effort, culminating in "a rich reward in heaven." As we say today, "no pain, no gain." Moral health will always be assailed by temptations—"I can resist anything except temptation," said Oscar Wilde—but self-discipline can prevail. It takes work, commitment, practice. But self-discipline is not a solitary enterprise. The Holy Spirit is there to support, guide, and teach us as we develop our Christian values.

Self-discipline starts with faith in the God who gives us life and a charter for living the "good life." It culminates with a strength of character that radiates virtue. "You must stand for something or you will fall for anything," says a familiar aphorism. What do you stand for? What steps are you willing to take to turn your values into character? What sacrifices do you have the courage to make to become the kind of person Jesus called to service? Discipline your actions to conform to noble values.

R_x 5.
Learn Morality from the Teaching and Examples of Good People

In Luke's Gospel, Jesus is shown as one who "grew in wisdom and stature and in favor with God and men." Jesus is the beneficiary of a sound moral education. We see him nurtured by loving earthly parents who accept him, love him, are grateful for him, and worry about him when he is "lost" in Jerusalem. In the temple he is welcomed and supported from his infancy forward by devoted religious teachers like Simeon and Anna. When his parents find the boy Jesus in the temple, he is surrounded by teachers who test him on his knowledge of religious law and engage him in moral exercises of asking and answering questions. Jesus no doubt learned from his mother's example of humility and his father's disciplined work life that God expects humans to grow by precept and practice—but also by choosing worthy examples to follow.

As imperfect as our own society is in the realm of moral health, we know that moral education begins early and at home. Some of that education (like John the Baptist's) is preventive and protective: keeping children away from values that corrupt. Parents may need to monitor friends and censor television: ours is the age of information overload, instant gratification, and "net surfing." The v-chip has come none too soon. But parents and teachers continue to be positive sources of moral education, too, for children learn what they live—at home and school.

Robert Fulghum captured this moral health prescription well in his popular book, *All I Really Need to Know I Learned in Kindergarten*. What he learned is not far removed from John the Baptist's moral code. Fulghum said of his own experience, "all I really need to know about how to live and what to do and how to be I learned in kindergarten. Wisdom was not at the top of the graduate-school mountain, but there in the sandpile at Sunday School."* There he learned such values as fair play, consideration of others, and honesty. Moral education, he implies, is important, and it has to start "in the sandpile."

Albert Einstein once observed, "it is easier to denature plutonium than to denature the evil spirit of man." The Holy Spirit, Luke assures us, can help us resist the evil temptations of Satan to live by the false standards of the good life that seem so natural in human society. Such resistance is largely a matter of education in virtue. Teach your children well! As adults, look to other adults who exemplify moral integrity and courage. Become the best exemplar of ethical behavior you can be as a beacon for others to follow.

---

* *All I Really Need to Know I Learned in Kindergarten: Uncommon Thoughts on Common Things* (New York, Villard Books, 1988, p. 6).

R_x 6.
Develop an Internal Moral Barometer

A wounded Confederate soldier once observed, "I asked God for strength that I might achieve; I was made weak that I might learn humbly to obey." Only the humble can open their hearts to the Holy Spirit; only the humble can develop the integrity of an *internal* moral barometer. Such a barometer will measure the congruence of thought and action and help heal the divided self. It offers an antidote to a major spiritual illness—hypocrisy. In Luke's diagnosis, the source of spiritual illness is pride. Pride is what makes it nearly impossible for humans to be humble. A Jewish proverb says, "pride is the mask of one's own faults." Another apt saying goes, "pride is the flower that grows in the devil's garden."

Luke uses the moral code of the Pharisees as a negative example of an *external* concept of morality. The Pharisees knew and observed all of the requirements of the Law of Moses—with the minute regulations and rituals developed to an exacting fine art. But without a real love for God and a spirit of humility, Jesus declared, no Pharisee could be truly moral. All he could do was to give to the world a show of morality. To the Pharisees Jesus said, "You are those who justify yourselves in the sight of others; but God knows your hearts" (16:15). From such divided selves is hypocrisy born. A modern definition of the hypocrite speaks to this "two-faced" morality: a hypocrite is someone who complains about all the sex and violence—playing on his VCR.

How does one develop an internal moral barometer? The ethic espoused by Jesus calls for an opening of the heart to the Holy Spirit, praying humbly for God's power to meet confessed need, responding boldly and consistently in acts of loving service wherever it is needed. This is why one law of love—love God, love your neighbor—working from the inside out can replace all of the external codes people have designed to control moral behavior. Simple in concept, extraordinarily difficult in practice. Work to internalize principles of ethical behavior so that you can make sound moral judgments in any situation.

****

Some people who want to lose weight check out all the diet books in the library; they know all they need to know about cholesterol, food exchanges, and "fat-burners." But until they put their knowledge into practice, they will not lose a single ounce. So it is with shaping up your moral character: put love to work.

There may be no better place to see morality at work in accordance with the law of love than in the practical world of financial management. Dr. Luke has much to say about financial health. What decisions we make about our resources—spiritual as well as fiscal—will tell others much about our character, values, and integrity. We turn now to Luke's teaching about "true riches."

CHAPTER 5

FINANCIAL HEALTH

"Money often costs too much."
—Ralph Waldo Emerson

While the Bible contains about 500 verses on prayer and slightly fewer than that on faith, it has over 2,000 verses on money. Jesus said more about money than any other given topic—much of it in the book of Luke. As a physician, Luke saw the misunderstanding and mismanagement of riches as a human illness. This illness was one more impediment to the full power of the Holy Spirit. Many of Luke's insights deal with financial definitions: What is "wealth"? Who is "rich"? What is the proper use of "money"? Where do people go wrong in the getting and spending of "income"? Luke addresses all of these questions as he ministers to the economic illness endemic to human nature. And he raises this most important financial question for us to answer: "If then you have been not faithful with the dishonest wealth, who will entrust to you the true riches?" (16:11).

Luke uses parables to convey most of Jesus' teaching about wealth. Consider the messages about a healthy perspective on possessions in the parables below.

Jesus and Financial Health
The Rich Fool

As Luke records the story, following his conflict at dinner with his host—one of the Pharisees about whom Jesus claimed "inside you are full of greed and wickedness" (11:40)—Jesus told the crowds they were "of more value than many sparrows" (12:6). At that point a man cried out, asking for help in getting his share of the family inheritance. Jesus replied: "Take care! Be on your guard against all kinds of greed; for one's life does not consist in the abundance of possessions" (12:15). He followed this pronouncement with an illustrative parable:

> "The land of a rich man produced abundantly. And he thought to himself, 'What should I do, for I have no place to store my crops?' Then he said, 'I will do this: I will pull down my barns and build larger ones, and there I will store all my grain and my goods. And I will say to my soul, "Soul, you have ample goods laid up for many years; relax, eat, drink, be merry."' But God said to him, 'You fool! This very night your life is being demanded of you. And the things you have prepared, whose will they be?' So it is with those who store up treasures for themselves but are not rich toward God" (12:16-21).

In the event his message was not crystal clear, Jesus said to his disciples: "I bid you put away anxious thoughts about food to keep you alive and clothes to cover your body. Life is more than food, the body more than clothes. Think of the ravens: they neither sow nor reap; they have no storehouses or barn; yet God feeds them. You are worth far more than the birds!" (12:22-24, NEB).

In this parable, Jesus addressed both mental health and financial health, for they are closely connected. The rich fool had an economic demon, and it caused him much mental stress. His wealth had become an obsession, a matter of constant preoccupation, a concern that created a state of anxiety. The man's money caused him to become spiritually myopic as he looked only at himself and at the present. That is nearsightedness at its worst. Notice how many times in this story he used the words *I* and *my*. Notice that he did not see beyond the night ("this very night your life is being demanded of you") when his money would have no value to him.

Notice how he had forgotten that behind all the abundant crops is God, the giver of all good possessions. His economic anxiety was actually impoverishing the quality of his spiritual life.

God called the rich man "a fool," a man lacking reason, understanding, sanity. This rich fool thought value was measured by possessions. He never understood that man does not live by bread alone, that his solution to having so much lay in giving more and storing less, that taking life easy and enjoying himself was a waste of human resources, and that happiness never comes from hoarding. Furthermore, he was not aware that gratitude rather than greed is the proper response to blessings received, that his spirit was dominated by his riches, and that security can never be purchased by money. His entire focus was on his goods, built up by years of economic striving, but he could not possess his life for even one more day. Yes, this rich man was a fool to let himself be owned by wealth and to believe that he could secure his own future. Such a man, Jesus taught, is poor indeed.

The rich fool put his trust in things rather than in God. He preferred riches he could touch to the unseen treasures of heaven and "became a pauper in the sight of God." What God had in store for him was not bigger barns but a burial. And then of what value was all his acquired wealth? Money only weighs down the casket.

Jesus told his disciples to learn from the negative example of the rich fool. Do not be anxious, do not worry, "but seek his [God's] kingdom, and these things will be given to you as well" (12:31, NIV). As is so characteristic of Luke's understanding of the gospel, Jesus told his disciples to have faith in the sufficiency of the Holy Spirit to supply all of their needs:

"Do not be afraid, little flock, for it is your Father's good pleasure to give you the kingdom. Sell your possessions, and give alms. Make purses for yourselves that do not wear out, an unfailing treasure in heaven, where no thief comes near and no moth destroys. For where your treasure is, there your heart will be also" (12:32-34).

A person may be a millionaire and yet spiritually bankrupt. Where *is* your treasure? Your spiritual health depends on how you answer that question.

Lost Goods

While the rich fool lost his life by trying to hold on to it, Luke relates three other connected parables that speak to the value of things lost and found. The three parables constitute the whole of chapter 15 and are told by Jesus when the scribes and Pharisees grumbled because Jesus was talking with "tax collectors and sinners" (15:1-2). In all three parables, the emphasis is on the agony of the one who lost something of value and the joy in finding it once again. Jesus knew that the Pharisees had written off sinners as lost and therefore worthless. In this triptych of parables, Jesus set forth God's standard of value.

The "parables of lost things" are three scenes in the economics of heaven. Each scene represents a good with a different value. To see the three parables in their connected context, examine the chart below:

Parables of Lost Things

What, specifically?	sheep	coin	son
What, generally?	animal	object	person
Where?	wilderness	house	far country
Value?	medium	low	high
Status of owner?	middle class	poor	wealthy
Why lost?	stupidity	carelessness	choice
Why sought?	responsibility	value	love

Now, let us look at each parable for its comment on economic health.

1) The Lost Sheep

The first parable is succinctly presented as scene one in

the triad of parables depicting lost things worth saving:

> "Which one of you, having a hundred sheep and losing one of them, does not leave the ninety-nine in the wilderness and go after the one that is lost until until he finds it? When he has found it, he lays it on his shoulders and rejoices. And when he comes home, he calls together his friends and neighbors, saying to them, 'Rejoice with me, for I have found my sheep that was lost.' Just so, I tell you, there will be more joy in heaven over one sinner who repents than over ninety-nine righteous persons who need no repentance" (15:3-7).

For shepherds, sheep were extremely valuable. Fleece was produced as a major commodity for the marketplace. Because the shepherd's primary responsibility was to keep the sheep together and protected from wolves, the one sheep which thoughtlessly wanders off was a matter of great concern to the shepherd.

Tending sheep was hard and dangerous work. It was also dirty and lonely work. Shepherds were not high in the socioeconomic status of the day, and yet the economy of agrarian Judea depended on the produce from the flock. The temple sacrifice of lambs symbolized the value sheep had in Jesus' time. Indeed, in an ironic way the sheep were considered more valuable than the shepherd. The lost sheep in this parable represented but 1% of the herd of 100—but the stupid beast, unaware of its danger in wandering from the flock, created an occasion for great joy when the searching shepherd discovered the lost sheep. It was in the job description of the shepherd to find lost sheep.

Jesus called himself the "good shepherd." He cared for every sheep under his care. He knew the voice of every sheep. He was distressed when an ignorant individual wandered away from the fold in search of greener pastures. He was a searcher after every lost sheep and rejoiced when the lost one was found. Were the ninety-nine "good" sheep of lesser value? No. But Jesus, good shepherd that he was, would go to any lengths to find the one who was lost. The sinner, outside the fence, was an individual Jesus reached out to as a valuable soul *worth* saving.

2) The Lost Coin

In the second scene in this triad, Jesus pointed out the value of a lost coin:

> "Or what woman, having ten silver coins, if she loses one of them, does not light a lamp, sweep the house, and search carefully until she finds it? When she has found it, she calls together her friends and neighbors saying, 'Rejoice with me, for I have found the coin that I had lost.' Just so, I tell you, there is joy in the presence of the angels of God over one sinner who repents"(15:8-10).

The actual value of a Greek silver drachma by our standards was probably not much. But for a peasant woman in Palestine, such a coin would be considered valuable—about a day's wages for that time. Without it, the family might not eat.

There could be another element of value in this story. A married woman in that culture wore headdresses with ten such silver coins on a silver chain. This was a symbol of her marriage and her value as a wife. To have lost one of these coins would mean far more than the monetary value. And in a dark Palestinian home where the floor of dried reeds and leaves could easily hide a lost coin, the discovery of the lost coin would bring the woman exceptional happiness. In this symbolic measure of value, the coin represented 10% of her possessions.

God, Jesus suggested in this parable, rejoices as did the woman when he finds a valuable person who has become lost among the common surroundings of hearth and home.

3) *The Lost Son*

The Parable of the Prodigal Son, the third scene of the trilogy, is one of the best-known and best-loved stories in the Bible. It is a powerful parable about love for those lost:

Again, he said: "There was a man who had two sons. The younger of them said to his father, 'Father, give me the share of the property that will belong to me.' So he divided his property between them. A few days later the younger son gathered all he had and traveled to a distant country, and there he squandered his property in dissolute living" (15:11-13).

As the familiar story played out, the younger son—now in dire straits—ended up slopping pigs, came to his senses, returned home to beg forgiveness for sinning against God and his father, and was welcomed with open arms by his father who saw him "while he was still far off." From his joyous father he received kingly treatment: a robe, a ring, shoes, the fatted calf, a feast— "for this son of mine was dead and is alive again; he was lost and is found" (15:14-24).

While the value of the sheep and the coin were great, the value of the lost son was beyond calculation. He represented 50% of the father's most precious possession; he was a human son who had deliberately gotten himself lost but came to his senses. The cash he inherited was not critical. What was important was that a soul had been saved. That was Jesus' response to the Pharisees' grumbling about his eating with sinners: God places value on every person and rejoices when sinners come back from wasted lives and worldly values to humble themselves in a return to the Father's heavenly household. By his repentance and humility, the younger son found favor with the father and was welcomed into the house; by his anger and self-righteousness, the older son found himself still outside the house—so like the proud, sullen, petty Pharisees sitting in judgment of Jesus.

In the kingdom of heaven, economic values are measured

in degrees of humility and repentance, not in amounts of money. Perhaps it is this sense that Jesus can declare that the first will be last. The basic economic question remains: "What good is it for a man to gain the whole world, and yet lose or forfeit his very self?" (9:25). The prodigal had learned that lesson in a "distant country." The elder brother was still focused on worldly definitions of the good and the valuable, thinking he had somehow *earned* his inheritance and his father's favor. A victim of economic illness of his day, he thought by his works and rituals he deserved to be wealthy. But by God's standard of value he was poor in spirit and ungrateful for grace.

The Rich Man and the Steward

In the story of the rich man and the steward, a puzzling parable for many Bible scholars, Jesus continued his teaching on financial health. Luke places this parable immediately after the Parable of the Prodigal Son, and it, too, raises points about the proper use of wealth.

The story line is this:

> "There was a rich man whose manager was accused of wasting his possessions. So he called him in and asked him, 'What is this I hear about you? Give an account of your management, because you cannot be manager any longer.' The manager said to himself, 'What shall I do now? My master is taking away my job. I'm not strong enough to dig, and I'm ashamed to beg—I know what I'll do so that, when I lose my job here, people will welcome me into their houses'" (16:1-4, NIV).

To deal with his economic distress, the manager called in his master's debtors and demanded immediate payment, giving each a discount on the debt. The master "commended the dishonest manager because he had acted shrewdly." Jesus drew this lesson from the parable: "I tell you, use worldly wealth to gain friends for yourselves so that when it is gone, you will be welcomed into eternal dwellings" (16:8-9, NIV).

Jesus attached three additional lessons to the first: (1) "Whoever can be trusted with very little can also be trusted with much." (2) "So if you have not been trustworthy in handling worldly wealth, who will trust you with true riches?" (3) "You cannot serve both God and money." Luke concludes this scene by observing that, "The Pharisees, who loved money, heard all this and were sneering at Jesus." Jesus responded, "You are the ones who justify yourselves in the eyes of men, but God knows your hearts. What is highly valued among men is detestable in God's sight" (16:10-15, NIV).

This unusual parable has been called "A Bad Man's Good Example" (William Barclay), "Shrewd Saints" (Lloyd Ogilvie), and "Two Rogues" (Campbell Morgan). Obviously, it was directed at the Pharisees "who loved money," but it was also an object lesson for the disciples. What does this parable tell us about financial health and spiritual wealth?

First, it tells us that where there is money there is corruption. Great riches always bring great temptations. The manager was not managing the master's resources responsibly and in the best interest of the master. He was "squandering" the money, perhaps spending it on his own needs or skimming from the profits of investments. The Pharisees were, in effect, no better than the prodigal son, for they hoarded and wasted on themselves God's spiritual capital of grace. Usury was forbidden in Jewish law, but the manager might not have cared much about such requirements for ethics and honesty. Given a choice between loyalty to his master and love for his master's money, he chose money. We always have a choice. What choice do we make?

Second, the parable tells us that those who are caught up in the financial values of the world—making and spending money—are often more dedicated to success and more calculating in their strategies than are those who work for the kingdom of God. Or so Jesus seemed to suggest. The master was impressed by his manager's resourcefulness, shrewdness, and brainpower. Too weak to dig and too proud to beg, the manager used the financial resources of his master to ensure himself friends to care for him when he was out of work. He turned his crisis into an opportunity.

Third, the parable tells us that life constantly tests how wisely we use the resources God has given us for his benefit. Luke embeds several test questions in the parable and they require a response. From God's point of view, are we good investments? What will our account books show about how we used God's capital? Luke reminds us that the wealth of this world is an illusion. We own nothing because everything is on loan. Can we be trusted to manage these resources responsibly? Honestly? Wisely? Do we keep money in its proper place, or do we let it control our values and decisions? Worldly wealth is not real, but it tests us at every turn. How do we do on the wealth test? Has our spending brought us closer to God? If you were arrested and charged with being a Christian, would your checkbook stubs convict you?

The Rich Young Ruler

Luke, like Matthew and Mark, tells us the story of Jesus' response to "a certain ruler." (In Matthew's account [19:16-26] he is young and rich.) The man asked Jesus, "What must I do to inherit eternal life?" After claiming to have followed the commandments, the young ruler was challenged with a final command from Jesus. As Luke tells the story, Jesus said:

> "There is still one thing lacking. Sell all that you own and distribute the money to the poor, and you will have treasure in heaven; then come, follow me." But when he heard this, he became sad; for he was very rich. Jesus looked at him and said, "How hard it is for those who have wealth to enter the kingdom of God! Indeed, it is easier for a camel to go through the eye of a needle than for someone who is rich to enter the kingdom of God." Those who heard it said, "Then who can be saved?" He replied, "What is impossible for mortals is possible for God" (18:18-27).

In his last lesson on wealth before he left for his final journey to Jerusalem, Jesus underscored again the new economic principle of the kingdom.

Here, a good man with high status and abundant wealth asked the same question that Jesus earlier answered with the Parable of the Good Samaritan. To inherit eternal life, Jesus suggested, is not merely a matter of following the law or being a good person. To inherit eternal life—perhaps the definition of "the true riches" (16:11)—requires a generous, giving spirit. This was precisely the spirit the young ruler lacked. In all likelihood, Jesus sensed that this man was actually owned by his wealth, that he truly loved his money, that he had made possessions his real God and thus his idol. So wedded was the young ruler to material things, and the comfort and joy they brought him, that he could not part with them even for the prize of eternal life.

The rich young ruler chose money over God. However, in the economics of salvation, value is measured by what one gives away for the welfare of others. The seduction of material wealth is that it shackles humans to this world with such a strong hold on their loyalty that putting God first becomes virtually impossible—as difficult as it might be for a camel to go through the eye of a needle.

There are two other observations worth making. First, when Luke refers to the "eye of a needle," he uses the Greek word for a *surgical* needle. How like a physician to use a term from his own profession. Second, the "eye of the needle" was the name used for a gate into Jerusalem used by beasts of burden. This was a small entrance that required the mighty camel to go through on his knees with his transported possessions removed from his back. Perhaps this was the very image Jesus had in mind for those who would enter the gates of heaven: kneeling and bereft of all baggage. As the Spanish proverb puts it, "There are no pockets on a shroud."

A Repentant Tax Collector

When Jesus made his way to Jerusalem at the time of

Passover, for what he knew would be his date with death, he attracted large and curious crowds. Luke describes an occasion in Jericho where Zacchaeus, a wealthy and hated tax collector, could not see Jesus because of the throng and so climbed a sycamore tree. Jesus spotted him and said, "Zacchaeus, hurry and come down, for I must stay at your house today." He welcomed Jesus into his home and, in sharp contrast to the rich young ruler, repented and volunteered to give half of his possessions to charity and to pay back four times over anyone he had cheated. The crowds questioned Jesus' willingness to associate with such disreputable and despised sinners. But Jesus responded, "Today salvation has come to this house" (19:1-10).

The Pounds

While still in Jericho, Jesus told one of his most revealing economic parables, a story quite similar to an historical event. Some years earlier, Archelaus, to whom Judea had been willed by his father Herod the Great, who died in 4 B.C., left his palace in Jericho and journeyed to Rome to convince Emperor Augustus to let him have his inheritance. The Jews hated Archelaus and sent a delegation of fifty of their own leaders to Rome to tell Augustus they did not want Archelaus as their king. While Augustus confirmed the inheritance, Archelaus returned to Jericho denied his royal title.

Luke relates this historically-based parable told by Jesus:

He said, "A nobleman went to a distant country to get royal power for himself and then return. He summoned ten of his slaves, and gave them ten pounds, and said to them, 'Do business with these until I come back.' But the citizens of his country hated him and sent a delegation after him, saying, ' We do not want this man to rule over us.' When he returned, having received royal power, he ordered these slaves, to whom he had given the money, to be summoned so that he might find out what they had gained by trading" (19:12-15).

What the king found was that one servant had invested very wisely and made ten pounds for his master, a second had invested well and made five pounds for his master, but a third servant had merely hidden the money in a cloth because he knew the master to be "a harsh man." To the first, the master gave ten cities to govern, to the second he gave five cities to govern, but to the third he said, "Why did you not put my money into the bank? Then when I returned, I could have collected it with interest" (19:16-23).

The man of noble birth then took the one pound from the servant who did not invest it and gave it to the man with ten. Jesus drew this moral from the parable: "To all those who have, more will be given; but from those who have nothing, even what they have will be taken away" (19:26).

Unlike the Parable of the Talents, where each servant receives a different allocation, this parable has the master giving every servant the same amount to invest: one pound. He was, we might say today, an equal opportunity employer. Each of the ten servants was given about ten dollars to take care of for the employer, specifically, to invest or trade in the world of business. The pound might represent the gift of faith, the gospel message, or the ministry gifts God gives each of us. Perhaps the pound is simply the gift of an individual life; every person receives only one such "resource" to invest for God's profit. In any event, what is important here, for Luke and us, is the principle of risk and return.

In this parable, the question is how bold, how intelligent, how shrewd is the servant in using his gift for the benefit of the master? There is no return without risk, a message Jesus seems to direct to his followers in the crowd. What do the disciples know about boldness for the kingdom? Do they have faith in the spiritual market, or do they fear the consequences of courageous and intelligent investing? Are they going to shrink back because they know Jesus is "a harsh man," or are they going to multiply their spiritual gifts by hard work and shrewd decisions? Luke underscores again the importance of fearless, bold courage by the servants—Jesus' disciples—if they are to become financially healthy in the "goods" of the kingdom of heaven.

The servant who lost his financial resources was guilty of not doing anything with what he had been given. In the economics of heaven, the responsible person finds ways to use his worth for the benefit of God. The reward for a life well spent is greater opportunity for service in the kingdom because "to all those who have, more will be given."

For Luke, financial resources are always a potential snare for the unsuspecting soul. Wealth is a disease that incapacitates because it so easily becomes the focus of one's love and loyalty. It blinds the spiritual eye to the needs of others, and it creates a false sense of security. Money and possessions, Luke wants to make clear, do not constitute "the true riches."

Real wealth is spiritual. It frees us to serve and to share. It keeps us working for the master and the kingdom. It does not shackle humans to this world but enables them to give, to risk, and to invest, all for the welfare of all those in need. In so doing, we may find true riches: eternal life—with "purses that do not wear out and never ending treasures in heaven."

DR. LUKE'S PRESCRIPTIONS
FOR FINANCIAL HEALTH

"I don't think you can spend yourself rich."
—George Humphrey

In the contemporary world, financial well-being is a major preoccupation for young and old. Most college students in the United States, surveys confirm, think the primary value of a college degree lies in economic advantage rather than in the pursuit of knowledge or the development of mind and character. Tax policies and economic promises continue to influence presidential and other elections for the working public.

Concerns about welfare for the poor and Medicare for the "baby boomer" generation dominate the news and editorial pages in the popular press. IRAs, NAFTA, downsizing, 401(k)s, mutual funds, Federal Reserve policy, inflation, depression, stagnation—these are the issues that raise the anxieties and blood pressures of an American public that is increasingly fixated on matters financial.

Consider a few frightening financial statistics reported in 1996, a year marking a generally positive five-year period of economic expansion in the United States:

- Economic growth has been modest (about 5% a year) and continuing layoffs keep consumers nervous

- Restructuring of 100 of America's largest companies from 1978 to 1996 resulted in 3 million layoffs—22% of the workforce in these companies—with 77% of the layoffs white-collar workers

- The United States trade deficit in 1995 was 174 billion dollars; the accumulated trade deficit in the last decade is over one trillion dollars

- Worker buying power is declining, after adjusting for inflation

- Forecasters predict a slumping economy reverting to about 2% growth. (Net national savings average less than 5% of the nation's output, down from the 11% average of the 1960s

- Net business investment is languishing at only 2% of GDP

- Social Security is headed toward bankruptcy over the next two decades unless major changes (such as privatization, means testing, and raising the retirement age) are adopted

- Increases in Medicare and Medicaid spending have been about 9%, and Medicare could soon be bankrupt without major changes

- Federal deficits, not including Social Security, have risen from their 1960s average of 0.9% of GDP to 4.2%

Even in a generally sound economic era—in 2000 the Dow is strong and deficits are being replaced by surplus—financial fears can focus our attention on material welfare, money, and economic security. It has ever been so. Luke in his prescriptions for spiritual health recognizes this universal human illness—storing up treasures on earth—and recommends these remedies:

R_x 1.
Do Not Be Owned by Your Money

Money, it is said, makes a good servant but a poor master. Luke saw that the Pharisees loved money, and he saw how that contributed to their preoccupation with self—self-righteousness, self-aggrandizement, self-sufficiency. Their money did not make them more spiritual but, rather, more elitist; not more holy but more arrogant. The Parable of the Rich Fool illustrated perfectly how wealth can lead to obsession with the accumulation of things. The rich man was controlled by his produce and spent his days contemplating larger storehouses. He thought he was building a secure future. He was wrong.

A popular and perverse modern rendition of "The Golden Rule" says, "Those who have the gold rule." But what do they rule? Like King Midas, they might rule over gold which cannot satisfy their true needs. You will recall that everything Midas touched turned to gold. One cannot eat gold. Or perhaps they rule over the diminishing kingdom of the self. When money owns us, we lose perspective on more important things, and our world becomes smaller and meaner. We focus on interest rates and trading deadlines, and worry over every downturn in the market. Do not let yourself be owned by your money—or you will become a pauper in the sight of God.

R_x 2.
Choose God Over Money

Luke recognized the role of choice in the spiritual development of humans. We can choose to be fearful or faithful, to worry or put away anxious thoughts, to spend our resources wastefully or wisely, to hide our pound in a handkerchief or invest in it shrewdly, to consider a layoff as a crisis or an opportunity, to worship money or God. Throughout his Gospel, Luke cited example after example of those who made the wrong choice: the rich fool, the prodigal son, the rich young ruler.

But there are also those who chose God: the prodigal son (when he came to his senses), Zacchaeus, the rich man's steward, and the servant who invested one pound wisely and made ten more. These were individuals of varying "worth" in the eyes of the world, but they found spiritual health by choosing God over money. You cannot choose both: "You cannot serve both God and money." As Luke recorded Jesus' prescription, "Strive for [God's] kingdom, and these things will be given to you as well" (12:31). Why choose God? Because, Jesus said, "It is your Father's good pleasure to give you the kingdom" (12:32). That is your wealth to secure spiritual health. Choose wisely: choose God.

R_x 3.
Invest in the Kingdom

Spiritual coin produces spiritual dividends. What, really, do we have to invest? There is the classic triad: time, talent, treasure. Where will such resources do the most good for the soul? For Luke, the answer was clear: invest in the work of God. There is a modern saying that applies here. It states, "Work for the Lord; the pay isn't much but the retirement plan is out of this world." Precisely. One of the most beautiful passages in the New Testament is in Jesus' admonition to the disciples about God's providence for the birds and the lilies: "Therefore I tell you, do not worry about your life, what you will eat, or about your body, what you will wear. For life is more than food, the body more than clothing" (12:22-23).

Jesus' investment strategy is heavenly. He told the disciples to "Sell your possessions, and give alms. Make purses for yourselves that do not wear out, an unfailing treasure in heaven, where no thief comes near, and no moth destroys" (12:33-34). Such an investment strategy affirms that "in God we trust." Investing in worldly markets is always risky, always anxiety-producing, because no one knows for sure what the markets will do. Mark Twain advised, "There are two times in a man's life when he shouldn't speculate: when he can afford to and when he can't." Luke reminded us that we can always count on a spiritual return from an investment in the kingdom. We cannot afford *not* to invest our time, talent, and treasure in stock sure to return rich dividends for spiritual health. Invest in the kingdom of God.

R_x 4.
Value Your Spiritual Health

Luke, good physician that he is, pointed out the value spiritual health has in God's economic scheme. Economics, after all, is concerned with values, the worth of anything. What value do we place on our spiritual well being? In his three related parables on "lost goods," Luke reminded us that the value of something can be measured by the joy one has in finding it. A lost sheep is valuable to the shepherd who is responsible for it. A lost coin is valuable to the woman who misplaced it. A lost son is valuable to the father who lets him go with his inheritance in hand.

Spiritual health, Luke suggested, is more valuable than any material possession. Your spiritual health *is* your wealth. Animals and objects and even children may be lost. But spiritual values are measured by the joy one has in finding something (or someone) thought to be gone forever. God's joy is particular and individual. Just as he is concerned with every bird and every flower, so is he concerned with every person—indeed, even more so. God gives individuals free will, opportunities to choose priorities, but he rejoices when that choice is for kingdom values. He wants to trust us with "the true riches." Make your choices reflect God's concepts of worth.

R_x 5.
Use It or Lose It

When it comes to spiritual health, we should remember the old prescription: use it or lose it. The rich young ruler was challenged to give away his wealth to the poor if he really wanted to inherit eternal life. He could not bring himself to use his wealth generously for the benefit of others. Luke implied that this decision cost the young ruler eternal life. Zacchaeus was willing to use his financial resources, ill-gotten gains they might be, for charitable and honorable purposes. Luke implied his decision gained him salvation. The servant who kept his one pound in a cloth rather than invest it had his money taken away and given to the servant who used his money wisely in the market.

For spiritual health, we must use talents and resources to get interest on our investment. If a muscle is not exercised, it atrophies. If a mind is not challenged to think, it becomes dull. If the spiritual resources of love, hope, faith, patience, forgiveness are not applied in the marketplace of human affairs, the soul withers. To grow strong in spirit use your spiritual muscles for the welfare of others—and the kingdom.

R_x 6.
Give to Live

This economic principle of spiritual health summarizes the ones before it. In the economics of earth, we are taught to save: anyone without a 401(k), 403(b), IRA, company pension, annuity or government retirement program is considered a financial liability in society. "I don't think you can spend yourself rich," said George Humphrey. "A penny saved is a penny earned," said Benjamin Franklin. "Save for a rainy day," says an old proverb. But that is not Luke's economic advice for spiritual health.

In the book of Luke, the economics of spiritual health take a different tack altogether. He who would save his life must be willing to lose it; he who would be first must be last—and servant of all; one who witnesses for God should take nothing for the journey; anyone who wishes to be a disciple must leave self behind. As Luke recorded it, Jesus asks: "What does it profit them if they gain the whole world, but lose or forfeit themselves?" (9:25). If you want to live, give. Your spiritual bank account grows as you give yourself away. Jesus put it this way:

> "There is no one who has left house, or wife, or brothers, or parents, or children, for the sake of the kingdom of God, who will not get back very much more in this age, and in the age to come eternal life" (18:29-30).

100% investment of self in the kingdom of heaven is, in God's economy, the only way to spend yourself rich. We sometimes say, "give 'til it hurts." Luke's prescription says, "give 'til it helps—and heals."

****

Luke sees health as a matter of wholeness, and that includes the practical dimensions of life. There is no more practical activity for most of us than managing our resources. In the various parables on wealth, Luke gives special emphasis to the attitudes we should have about the role of riches in a healthy life. He warns readers of all eras: Do not let possessions undermine integrity. When wealth rules our value system, we develop divided loyalties, and no one can serve two masters. Financial health requires us to keep our loyalties, and our priorities, in proper order.

In the next chapter, we will see how Luke presents his notions of religious health as a condition of ultimate importance. For Luke, as so often is the case, Jesus' life and work create the ideal that instructs.

CHAPTER 6

RELIGIOUS HEALTH

*"Faith is building on what you know is here
so you can reach what you know is there."*
—Cullen Hightower

Throughout the book of Luke, health has been a concern close to the surface of the physician-author's mind. As Luke looked at prevailing religious principles and practices, he observed pathologies of worship needing a physician's healing hand. In the power of Jesus' pure understanding of God, Luke found the antidotes to religion gone awry. Luke traced the life and work of Jesus from conception to resurrection, and showed how Jesus exemplified a healthy religious regimen in all phases of his life. Such a regimen was displayed by what Jesus said and what he did, in the temple and on the road, with righteous saints and hypocrites and sinners, and from his humble birth to his horrible death and final departure to heaven.

The Religious Health of Jesus
The Early Years

In the birth narratives of John the Baptist and Jesus, Luke described the humility and receptivity of Elizabeth and Mary to the will of God and the work of the Holy Spirit in their lives. Both overcame fear and doubt by a quality of faith and gratitude for their blessings that reflected their calm confidence in God's power. And the shepherds too, when they heard the news of Jesus' birth from the angel of the Lord, in humble obedience overcame both terror and fear to follow the star to the manger in Bethlehem. Having seen the baby Jesus, they returned to their work in the fields "glorifying and praising God for all they had heard and seen" (2:20). These were the attitudes and actions Luke found to be religiously healthy.

As "Jesus grew in wisdom and stature, and in favor with God and men" (2:52, NIV), he worshiped in the temple. He had completed the required ceremonies of circumcision and purification as an infant, was endorsed by the devout temple worshipers Simeon and Anna, and, at the age of twelve, was found by his parents in the temple amazing the teachers by his intelligence and his understanding of Scripture. Baptized in the Jordan, Jesus was praying when "heaven was opened and the Holy Spirit descended upon him in bodily form like a dove, and a voice came from heaven, 'You are my beloved Son; with you I am well pleased'" (3:21-22). Then, at the age of about thirty, he began his teaching and healing ministry.

By *following* the traditions of his religion—ceremony, study, baptism, prayer—Jesus had prepared himself to receive the power of the Holy Spirit to undertake the challenges of teaching others the real meaning of the kingdom, the Messiah, and religious truth. Luke showed how religious traditions, rightly understood, grounded the faithful in sound practices and in values pleasing to God.

The Middle Years

During approximately three years of ministry, Jesus constantly confronted the pathological religious practices of his day. Practices that should have led individuals to the kind of worship exhibited by Mary, John the Baptist, Simeon, Anna, and Jesus himself had become for the people of his day ritualized, distorted, and empty of faith and power to help people see God. The scribes and Pharisees sanitized religious life and reduced it to the fruitless and futile attempt to follow their corrupted views of God's laws. The common folk of the day ignored the mandates of religion, and often found themselves rejected by religious leaders as condemned sinners. It was to this diverse audience that Jesus brought startling prescriptions for religious health.

In his short ministry traced by Luke, Jesus demonstrated by word and deed what a true understanding of God would do to enrich and empower life. By word, he reminded the righteous Jew what the law and the prophets actually required. He taught the disciples directly what the mission of the Messiah had to be. He told parables to his followers and his critics so that by such "earthly stories with heavenly meanings" he might communicate the essence of the religious life. By deed, he healed the sick and raised the dead to demonstrate the power of faith and the Holy Spirit. He ate with sinners and welcomed children, prostitutes, and the poor. He "worked" on the Sabbath and demonstrated the critical importance of putting service ahead of ceremony. For Jesus, the religious life is one of love, forgiveness, peace, work, joy, and self-sacrifice. This he called the "abundant life."

By *challenging* the traditions of his religion—which (as Luke saw it) had been reduced to formalized rituals and hypocritical life styles—Jesus presented the "good news" that God loved sinners and rejoiced at their repentance and return. People could never earn their way into eternal life on their own merits. As Jesus answered a question from the lawyers and Pharisees about why he ate with tax collectors and sinners, "It is not the healthy who need a doctor, but the sick. I have not come to call the righteous, but sinners to repentance" (5:30-32, NIV). Luke's contention was that to one degree or another everyone is ill—but only some realize it.

The Final Weeks

Jesus knew that his mission required him to challenge the religious leaders and corrupt religious practices of his day, and that such opposition to orthodoxy would result in his own demise. He tried time and again to teach his myopic, forgetful, dense disciples that the road to Jerusalem for Passover was a hard road to travel and that it was the destiny of the Messiah to die for his unpopular religious views.

Luke writes:

> Then he took the twelve aside and said, "See, we are
> going up to Jerusalem, and everything that is written
> about the Son of Man by the prophets will be accom-
> plished. For he will be handed over to the Gentiles; and
> he will be mocked, insulted, and spat upon. After they
> have flogged him, they will kill him, and on the third day
> he will rise again" (18:31-33).

Unfortunately, said Luke, the deafness of the disciples was
again at work: "But they understood nothing about all these
things; in fact, what he said was hidden from them, and they
did not grasp what was said" (18:34).

On the road to Jerusalem, by way of Jericho, Jesus met a
blind man who could see much better than the disciples, and
whose persistence in seeking Jesus' help for his blindness was
rewarded. Jesus said to him, "Receive your sight; your faith
has healed you" (18:42, NIV). And here is where he met
Zacchaeus, who proved himself worthier of salvation than
the rich young ruler. Soon Jesus began his entry into
Jerusalem on a colt he had arranged to have ready as he
neared the city. (A king entering a city on a colt symbolized an
emissary of peace.) Jesus wept because he knew Jerusalem
had not chosen the Prince of Peace—and that its destruction
by Rome (which actually happened in A.D. 70) was sure.

Although he came in peace, Jesus was to create continuing controversy by his bold confrontations with religious
leaders. One of the most remarkable confrontations, one only
briefly mentioned by Luke, was in the temple where, as Luke
describes it, he began driving out the traders with these
words: "It is written, 'My house shall be a house of prayer';
but you have made it a den of robbers" (19:45-46). This courageous action by Jesus was one more reason some of the religious leaders in Jerusalem "kept looking for a way to kill
him" (19:47).

In this incident, we can see how official religious practices had degenerated into a cancer on the kingdom of God. The High Priest Annas had established a profitable business in the outer court of the temple, the Court of the Gentiles. Here animals were sold for the required temple sacrifices and foreign money was exchanged—also at a handsome profit—into Jewish money on which the temple tax had to be paid. The chief priests ran a virtual monopoly, charging exorbitant fees that victimized the poor while enriching the business of religion. It was precisely this corruption of religion for financial gain that enraged Jesus and led to his courageous action in cleansing the temple. The purpose of the temple, he declared, was not profit but prayer.

As Luke's Gospel outlines the events, Jesus had carefully planned his final days. His entry was organized to fulfill messianic prophecies found in the Old Testament. The prophet Zechariah had said the Messiah would arrive humble and riding on an ass (see Zechariah 9:9 and Matthew 21:4-5). Psalm 118 had described the entry of the Lord accompanied by praise from the pilgrims as the deliverer: "The stone which the builders rejected has become the chief cornerstone" (see Psalm 118:22 and Luke 20:17). In the temple, Jesus declared himself master of his "house of prayer," fulfilling the prophecy of Malachi: ". . . the Lord whom you seek will suddenly come to his temple...; and he will purify the descendants of Levi and refine them like gold and silver, until they present offerings to the Lord in righteousness" (3:1-3). So, at last, Jesus took on official religion and challenged its leaders in the temple.

Within the Walls of the Temple

As he actively assumed the prophetic role of the Messiah, knowing full well that the self-interest of the priests would indeed lead them to reject the cornerstone, Jesus taught the good news to people in the temple and sparred with the scribes and Pharisees. In one encounter he told the Parable of the Vineyard.

Luke recounted this parable about the rejection of the Messiah in response to questions from religious leaders about

Jesus' authority to challenge religion within the walls of the temple itself. Jesus told the story this way:

"A man planted a vineyard, and leased it to tenants, and went to another country for a long time. When the season came, he sent a slave to the tenants in order that they might give him his share of the produce of the vineyard; but the tenants beat him and sent him away empty-handed. Next he sent another slave; that one also they beat and insulted and sent away empty-handed. And he sent still a third; this one also they wounded and threw out. Then the owner of the vineyard said, 'What shall I do? I will send my beloved son; perhaps they will respect him.' But when the tenants saw him, they discussed it among themselves and said, 'This is the heir; let us kill him so that the inheritance may be ours.' So they threw him out of the vineyard and killed him. What then will the owner of the vineyard do to them? He will come and destroy those tenants and give the vineyard to others" (20:9-16).

Because the religious leaders making up the Sanhedrin, the ruling body of the Jews, were trying to trap Jesus into a charge of blasphemy, he used the parable above as an indirect response to their questions. The leaders wanted to discredit Jesus' religious authority and legitimate his arrest. The Parable of the Vineyard was indirect but quite clear, requiring the religious authorities to draw the inescapable conclusion themselves: they were the ones guilty of heresy and blasphemy.

The vineyard was an Old Testament image frequently used by the prophets to represent Israel (For example, see Ps. 80:8-19, Is. 5:1-7, Jer. 12:10, Hos. 10:1). The man who planted the vineyard is God, the tenants left in charge are the religious leaders, the servants sent by the owner to collect his share of the produce are the prophets, and the "beloved son" is Jesus. There can be no doubt that Jesus here predicted his own death at the hands of the religious leaders and God's subsequent judgment on them and Israel. Embodied in this one short parable is the entire history of God's relationship with his people. It says much about God's purpose, patience, and persistence; it also speaks volumes about human perfidy.

In another attempt to trap Jesus, the religious leaders asked him, "Is it right for us to pay taxes to Caesar or not?" (20:22, NIV). Because the fanatical wing of the Jews objected to bowing to any king besides God, they had often, on religious principle, protested this tax to the Roman government. If they could get Jesus to protest this tribute, they could report him to Pilate to be arrested; if he supported the tax to the hated civil government, they could turn the people against him.

Jesus would not let himself be caught in an either/or, no-win response. Instead, he gave a both/and reply. He implied in this account that religious people live under civil government and have a responsibility to follow its laws and support it with taxes. But religious people are also subject to God's law and have a responsibility to abide by the precepts of heaven. The conscientious person will make the right decisions and will know how, honorably, both to respect the state and to follow the dictates of God. Jesus' advice, after looking at a Roman silver piece with Caesar's image on it, was to "give to Caesar what is Caesar's, and to God what is God's" (20:26, NIV). Again, as is often the case in Luke's Gospel, the answer was put back on the conscience of the religious leaders. Religious health means serving God with a pure and honest heart.

The Final Hours

Luke carefully chronicles the final hours in Jesus' life, describing events so that Theophilus (and other readers) would see the messianic prophecies being fulfilled. Following additional teaching in the temple—much of it predicting wars, insurrections, earthquakes, famines, plagues, and celestial portents leading up to a Day of Judgment. He advised the people to be on the alert, "praying that you may have the strength to escape all these things that will take place, and to stand before the Son of Man" (21:36). And so he was ready for

Passover and his final hours with his disciples.

Passover was the high point of the religious year for all Jews, and Jerusalem would have been crowded with thousands of Jewish pilgrims from near and far. Every male Jew of age who lived within 15 miles of Jerusalem was required to be in the city to celebrate this sacred commemoration of the deliverance of the Jews from captivity in Egypt. Every foreign Jew hoped to celebrate at least one Passover in Jerusalem. Peter and John were sent to arrange for the Passover meal Jesus would share with his disciples. Jesus had previously selected a house in the city, and a man "carrying a jar of water" would lead his disciples to "a large room upstairs" for the religious ritual of Passover. Jesus knew it was his last such meal with his followers, and he wanted it to reflect all of the new meaning he was trying to communicate about the nature of religious health.

Luke described the events of the Eucharist in vivid detail and arresting dialogue (22:17-34).

- Jesus took a cup of wine, gave thanks, and said, "Take this and divide it among yourselves."

- Jesus took a loaf of bread, gave thanks, broke it, gave it to them and said, "This is my body, which is given for you. Do this in remembrance of me."

- Jesus passed the cup again after supper, saying, "This cup that is poured out for you is the new covenant in my blood."

- Jesus then declared, "The one who betrays me is with me and his hand is on the table."

- Jesus settled a jealous "dispute" about which disciple was the greatest, saying, "the greatest among you must become like the youngest, and the leader like one who serves."

- Jesus then passed on the leadership to the disciples: "You are those who have stood by me in my trials; and I confer on you, just as my Father has conferred on me, a kingdom."

- Jesus ominously told Peter, who had insisted, "Lord, I am ready to go with you to prison and to death!" that "the cock will not crow this day until you have denied three times that you know me."

When the meal was over, Jesus and his disciples went out to the Mount of Olives, where he prayed: "Father, if you are willing, remove this cup from me; yet not my will but yours be done" (22:42).

In this last teaching opportunity, Jesus passed on to his disciples his most telling lessons yet on what was required for religious well being. As always in Luke's Gospel, he taught by word and deed.

First, he observed the religious traditions of the faith. To be in Jerusalem, the Holy City, for the Passover celebration was a mark of his commitment to the religious heritage that was his. The Passover meal was arranged and completed according to the requirements of Jewish law. Traditions have value for preserving religious health.

Second, he put himself personally into the substance of the celebration. The bread and wine were to be symbols of his atoning death—his very being—and for that he gave thanks to God. For religious traditions to live they must have the spirit of life itself at work in them.

Third, he reminded his disciples that all humans were flawed—by errors in judgment (Judas), by self-interest (the disciples seeking high rank), and by excesses in claims of courage (Peter). Religious health is possible for imperfect people.

Fourth, he acknowledged the importance of fidelity. Although dense of mind and flawed in character, the disciples ultimately held on to their commitment to Jesus. Religious health is marked by constancy when the world challenges the faithful.

Fifth, he put his life in God's hands. He prayed for what he hoped, but was ready to accept what God had in store for him: "Yet not my will but yours be done." The religious life that is healthy—that is, whole, unified, at peace—is the life in which the will of God prevails. For Christians of all eras, that requires a life given to the Holy Spirit through absolute faith in Christ as the only Son of God. In no other way can the Holy Spirit pervade and transform frail human hearts, minds, and souls.

Luke describes how Jesus, coming back from his prayer at Olivet, found the disciples asleep, worn out by grief. Jesus asked, "Why are you sleeping? Get up and pray that you may not come into the time of trial" (22:46). For those who had just inherited the mantle of religious leadership, there was no time for grief, nor even for sleep. For Luke, religion had to be active to be healthy. It was the time for courage, work, and prayer: Jesus was on the way to arrest, trial, and the cross.

Betrayed by Judas and soon to be denied by Peter, Jesus was arrested in the Garden of Gethsemane. He was mocked and insulted by his guards and brought the next day before the 71 elders, lawyers, Pharisees and Sadducees making up the Sanhedrin. Because the charge was one of blasphemy, the council could decide the religious question at issue. However, the religious leaders could not carry out a death sentence without a sanction from the Romans. What they needed was evidence that Jesus was a political threat to Rome: "Are you, then, the Son of God?" they asked, and Jesus said, "You say that I am" (22:70). His answer was a way of affirmation.

The Jewish leaders took Jesus to Pilate and opened the case against him by saying, "We found this man perverting our nation, forbidding us to pay taxes to the emperor, and saying that he himself is the Messiah, a king" (23:2). Although Jesus did admit, on occasion, to being the Messiah (see Matthew 16:13-17 and John 4:45-26), the other charges were blatantly false. Pilate tried to wash his hands of the decision by sending him to Herod Antipas, the Galilean governor. When Herod sent him back, Pilate tried to free him for lack of evidence for a capital punishment, to let him off with a flogging—but the leaders and the crowd shouted back, "Crucify, crucify him!" Luke says succinctly, "Their voices prevailed. So

Pilate gave his verdict that their demand should be granted" (23:6-24). For Luke the legal issues are clear: Jesus is innocent, but a few religious leaders will stop at nothing to get rid of him. Pilate is too cowardly to refuse their demands and so agrees to crucify an innocent man.

Encounters on the Cross

On his way to his crucifixion, Jesus encountered several individuals, all of whom learned something from him about religious health. There were the women who mourned and lamented. To them he said, "Daughters of Jerusalem, do not weep for me, but weep for yourselves and for your children" (23:28). There were those who carried out the crucifixion. To them he said, "Father, forgive them; for they do not know what they are doing" (23:34). There were the two criminals crucified with him. To one who defended him against taunts from the other, Jesus said, "Truly I tell you, today you will be with me in Paradise" (23:43). And there was Jesus alone with God at the moment of death. To him he said, "Father, into your hands I commend my spirit." Luke then adds, "Having said this, he breathed his last" (23:46).

In these brief encounters, Luke demonstrates how Jesus displayed the virtues of religious excellence: courage in conflict, compassion in crises, forgiveness in adversity, trust in matters eternal. In the realm of religion these are lessons for how to live and how to die. Jesus had prescriptions, Luke knew, for both aspects of the human journey. He died with a prayer on his lips.

Easter Experiences

The story does not end here. There was "a good and righteous man named Joseph, who, though a member of the council [Sanhedrin], had not agreed to their plan and action" [to arrest and try Jesus]. He took down Jesus' body from the cross, wrapped it in linen, and laid it in a "rock-hewn" tomb (23:50-53). Luke notes that it was Friday, the "day of Preparation," and the Sabbath was about to begin. The women who had come with Jesus from Galilee went home and prepared spices and perfumes for the burial and, after resting on the Sabbath as required by Jewish law, came to the tomb on Sunday. Amazingly, they found the large stone closing the tomb had been rolled away.

Appearing in "dazzling clothes" were two men who asked, "Why do you look for the living among the dead?" The men reminded the astonished women that Jesus had told them in Galilee "that the Son of Man must be handed over to sinners, and be crucified, and on the third day rise again." The women reported this experience to the disciples and others, but no one believed them (24:5-11).

Luke reports another experience on the same day. Two of the disciples were on the road to Emmaus, about seven miles from Jerusalem, talking about "all these things that had happened." As they walked and talked, "Jesus himself came near and went with them, but their eyes were kept from recognizing him" (24:13-16). He asked what they were debating and was chastised by one disciple for being "the only stranger staying in Jerusalem who does not know the things that have taken place there in these days?" (24:17-18). They summarized for Jesus his own trial, death, and reported disappearance from the tomb. Jesus responded, "Oh, how foolish you are, and how slow of heart to believe all that the prophets have declared!" (24:25). Then he explained to them how his life and death were referred to "in all the scriptures" (24:27).

In the last scenes in Luke, Jesus was persuaded to stay with the two disciples and to have a meal with them (at which time they finally recognized him). The two disciples rushed back to Jerusalem to tell the others what they had seen—and Jesus again appeared. The disciples again failed to recognize him until he explained the messianic mission and prophecy. He commissioned them to declare to all the nations "that repentance and forgiveness of sins is to be proclaimed in his name to all nations, beginning from Jerusalem" (24:27).

The religious well-being of the world now passed to the disciples. They would not be left without support for the challenging work of witnessing. Luke records Jesus' final words to the disciples: "I am sending upon you what my Father's promised; so stay here in the city until you have been clothed with power from on high" (24:49). He led them to Bethany, blessed them, and parted from them. The disciples, Luke concludes, "returned to Jerusalem with great joy; and they were continually in the temple glorifying God" (24:52-53).

They had heard the word. Now they were almost ready to act, to *do* the word of God. While waiting for the "power from on high," the gift of the Holy Spirit they will receive at Pentecost, they spend their time wisely by praising God.

DR. LUKE'S PRESCRIPTIONS FOR RELIGIOUS HEALTH

"God is a verb."
—Buckminster Fuller

What is the state of religious health in the United States today? If one reads the popular press and listens to televangelists, the prognosis is not so cheerful. Religion seems ever at the mercy of cultural decay. On the one hand, we hear about the rise of cults and the occult, radical fundamentalism and evangelical fanaticism, and "new age" spirituality. On the other hand, we hear about declining membership in mainline Protestant churches and widespread apathy (if not apostasy) among Catholics. In a popular book Stephen Carter of Yale University characterizes America as a *Culture of Disbelief*. Theological questions about such topics as abortion become major political issues while political questions about such topics as the separation of church and state are hotly debated from the pulpit. What diagnosis rings true?

In our time, pollsters have provided all manner of surveys to measure public opinion. Consider some of the statistical results of surveys conducted in the mid 1990s:

- Almost 95% of Americans say they believe in God
- About 80% believe in miracles, life after death, and the virgin birth of Jesus
- 65% say they believe in the devil and 72% believe in angels
- In a World Values Survey in 1990-93, 82% of U.S. respondents said they considered themselves religious, compared to 55% in Britain, 54% in western Germany, 48% in France
- In the same survey, 44% of Americans said they attended a religious service at least once a week, against 18% in western Germany, 14% in Britain, 10% in France, 4% in Sweden
- In 1998, church membership stood at about 70%. (Only 17% of Americans belonged to a church in 1776; by the Civil War era, that figure rose to 37%; by 1910 the figure increased to 50%)
- 55% of Americans today say they are very satisfied with their spiritual lives
- A Gallup survey found that of those with yearly earnings under $20,000, two out of three say religion is very important to them versus less than half of those earning $50,000 or more
- A poll commissioned by the international humanist magazine *Free Inquiry* found that 90% of Catholics and 85% of Protestants believe the soul goes to a higher level of existence after death
- In this same poll, 89% of respondents, including 97% of Protestants, believe in a personal God who can answer prayer

These statistics, to the extent they are accurate, might seem to suggest that the United States is in relatively good religious health—compared to other countries and even compared to its own history.

Other contemporary surveys cast a shadow over this positive diagnosis. For example, a poll by George Barna found that, yes, over 90% of Americans own a Bible but only 34% said they had read from it in the past week. That figure is down from 50% as recently as 1992. Barna concluded that the Bible is a great icon but not a source of advice or inspiration for most Americans. Furthermore, in analyzing data from 28 religion surveys between 1987 and 1996, he suggests America is changing from a Christian nation to a spiritually diverse society. One of the casualties of this transformation is knowledge of basic Bible content.

For example, the recent Barna survey produced such findings as these:

- 80% of Americans incorrectly think the Bible includes the statement, "God helps those who help themselves"

- 65% do not know what John 3:16 refers to (in spite of signs waved before television cameras at pro football games!)

- Only 50% of adults know that the book of Jonah is in the Bible

- 10% believe Joan of Arc was the wife of Noah

In some ways the religious pulse is strong in America; in other ways the patient is in need of emergency room care. What prescriptions does Dr. Luke provide to modern-day Christian disciples? Here are a few with promise:

R_x 1.
Start with Yourself

The admonition in Luke, "Doctor, cure yourself" (4:23) is apt advice for most of us. Too often, Christian disciples have not put their own houses on a sound foundation before starting to patch their neighbor's roof. Jesus' own foundation was built on rock, on religious training that was strong and true. We should follow that example. Jesus frequently reminded his disciples to work from the inside out, to be sure that the eye of the body was sound, to know the heart was pure, and to avoid judging others when there was fault to be found within the follower of Christ. He asked his disciples, "Why do you see the speck in your neighbor's eye, but don't notice the log in your own eye?" (6:42).

In a most insightful tombstone inscription in the crypts of Westminster Abbey, an Anglican bishop made this lament about his life:

> When I was young and free and my imagination had no limits, I dreamed of changing the world.
> As I grew older and wiser, I discovered the world would not change, so I shortened my sights somewhat and decided to change only my country.
> But it too seemed immovable.
> As I grew into my twilight years, in one last desperate attempt, I settled for changing only my family, those closest to me, but alas, they would have none of it.
> And now, as I lay on my deathbed, I suddenly realize: If I had only changed myself first, then by example I might have changed my family.
> From their inspiration and encouragement, I would then have been able to better my country, and who knows—I may have even changed the world.

Jesus called his disciples to a high standard of self-examination and self-improvement. This is the first step to religious health. Begin with honest appraisal of your sins, follow with contrition and repentance, conclude with a confession of faith that recognizes the exclusive Spirit-power of Jesus to change the world. Change yourself first.

R_x 2.
Pray and Worship in the Temple

While Jesus was a radical and a revolutionary, he was also the epitome of religious orthodoxy. Throughout his education he followed the tenets of Jewish faith, learned the Scriptures in great depth and detail, observed the rituals and ceremonies of Jewish tradition, studied with the rabbis in the temple, and always took his needs to God in sincere prayer. He advocated a humble spirit in prayer and taught his disciples how to pray. And while he prayed in the temple and taught others who gathered there what Scripture really meant, he also prayed in boats, on mountains, and on the cross.

Here was one of the great ironies of Jesus' ministry. Although he criticized religious leaders and challenged their understanding of religious truth, he never left the temple. So often, it seems, the contemporary Christian can find a good reason to avoid worship in the church. But perhaps that's the case in other areas of modern life as well. Consider the following set of excuses:

Twelve Reasons Why I Quit Going to Football Games

1. The stadium is so large that I don't see many people I know. No one ever speaks to me or greets me at the gate.

2. Saturday is the only day I have to sleep.

3. The seats are too hard.

4. I want to relax, but everybody expects me to get into the spirit of the game.

5. The coach never comes to call on me; he does not even recognize me on the street.

6. The coach expects too much of the players. He ought to be able to do the job himself. After all, that's what he is being paid for.

7. I don't like the rules of the game. They are too strict and outmoded. I think the players should be permitted to make up their own rules as they go along.

8. They're always asking for money!! It costs me every time I go, and even between games they sometimes come around asking for money.

9. The band and cheerleaders don't use all the old tunes and yells. They have too many new ones.

10. There are some people in the stands who just come to be seen. They aren't sincere (like I am).

11. I can listen to the game and get just as much out of it from radio or TV.

12. I've been to those games. If you've seen one, you've seen 'em all.

Why, one might think this a comment on Sunday worship as well! (Especially since this anonymous piece appeared in a church bulletin.) Make no excuses: Go to church where you can worship with others.

R_x 3.
Hear and Do the Word

Jesus talked to his disciples, told them parables, taught them how to pray, conversed with them on the road and at the table. He wanted them to know as much as possible—about God, heaven, the Messiah, and the principles of spiritual health. Their inability to hear clearly was a major challenge to his mission. So he used the teacher's tools to break through spiritual deafness: clear messages, vivid examples, concrete demonstrations, object lessons, engaging questions, exhortation, and repetition. To understand religious truth you must first *hear* it.

But hearing is never enough. Displaying some frustration, Jesus asked his disciples, "Why do you call me 'Lord, Lord,' and *do* not do what I tell you?" (6:46). And he defined his family this way: "My mother and my brothers are those who hear the word of God and *do* it" (8:21). Constantly, Jesus explains that he is a religious leader who manifests what he believes in what he does.

Consistently, Jesus told his audiences that they would be judged by the fruit they produced—by their actions not their promises. His instructions were filled with imperatives: follow me, go in peace, love one another, show faith, take up your cross, do that and you will live, pray, seek and you will find. Jesus declared, "Blessed are those who hear the word of God and obey it" (11:28). Perhaps this emphasis on *doing* the word is what leads Buckminster Fuller to say, "God is a verb." The essence of the Christian faith is this: Hear and do the word of God.

R_x 4.
Be an Example to Others

Religion, if it is healthy, shines through behavior. We say "values are caught not taught" and "what you are doing speaks so loudly I cannot hear what you are saying." We have also heard it said that "the smallest package in the world is a person all wrapped up in himself." In the religious life this is one reason why doing the word of God is essential. Hearing and doing are complementary activities—one internal and passive, the other external and active—that unite thought and action, word and deed, in the healthy soul. But the religious life is rarely lived successfully in isolation: a solitary Christian is a contradiction in terms. Healthy Christianity always gets us outside ourselves and the "small packages" we tend to become. We have churches and classes and fellowship so that the healing work of the Holy Spirit can work by contagion. So what kind of example to others is your religious life?

Jesus railed against negative religious exemplars. He chafed at the arrogance and elitism of the Pharisees and the intellectual rigidity of the scribes. No worse example of prayer can be found in Scripture than the pompous and self-satisfied Pharisee standing next to the humble publican. Jesus drove out the money changers who were making a house of prayer into a robbers' cave. No worse example of religion for profit can be discovered in the Bible. Even the disciples became poor examples for others when they demonstrated fear instead of faith—in the storm-tossed boat in the Sea of Galilee, and at the arrest of Jesus by the chief priests.

For positive examples of Christian virtues—love, faith, humility, and others—look first to Christ. He is the model for religious health. And then look at exemplary figures in

Scripture. Luke shows us humble sinners, brave sick people, forgiving fathers, serving mothers, honest stewards, intelligent home builders, faithful friends, confessing tax gatherers, and learning disciples. The list of good examples of the religiously happy is long. What kind of sermon are we? Be an example of your faith—a faith that frees you to love and a faith that unites you with Christ.

R_x 5.
Honor Church and State

One of the more difficult challenges for the contemporary Christian is finding the proper balance between life in the world and life in the spirit. These two spheres of life seem to make contrary demands on our very being. We may try to compartmentalize our time—Sunday for worship, November for voting, December for Christmas—but that does not easily solve the conflict we feel. So much money for taxes and so much for tithes. That, too, avoids the deeper conflict within the soul. Debates about abortion, school prayer, values education, and many other issues leave us feeling angry and confused—as paralyzed to act as the paralytic Jesus healed. What's a Christian to do?

Jesus knew that inner conflict and outer controversy between church and state were not healthy conditions. Even though he knew he was the Prince of Peace—and rode a colt into Jerusalem at Passover to emphasize that point—he understood his messianic mission was to be put to death by a strange coalition of religious and political leaders. This did not keep him from teaching the new principles of government for church and state:

- Every kingdom divided against itself goes to ruin.

- Love your enemies, pray for those who treat you spitefully.

- Pass no judgment and you will not be judged.

- Provide for yourselves...never-failing treasure in heaven.

- Pay Caesar what is due Caesar and pay God what is due God.

What is Caesar's and what is God's? No formula can answer that question. Jesus leaves us with a prescription for peace that requires each person to decide: how do I live honorably as a citizen of the state *and* a citizen of God's kingdom? For Jesus it is a both/and question. Honor church *and* state.

R_x 6.
Trust in the Goodness of God

Religious health ultimately requires total trust in the goodness of God. The conflicts that debilitate, the choices that paralyze, and the self-interest that afflicts the soul can never be resolved, decided, or healed by a person's own efforts. That is one of the central lessons in the search for religious health. People must ask, seek, knock; they must love, serve, forgive. They must pray, witness, give. They must attempt to do all of these things with bold humility. So the Gospel of Luke teaches. But they must never believe that they are the architects of the kingdom. They should think of themselves as patients in need of the healing power of the Holy Spirit.

In a February, 1996, newspaper article Associated Press Science Editor Daniel Q. Haney reported that physicians at Georgetown University reviewed 212 studies and found that three-fourths of them showed a positive effect of religious commitment on health. Religious faith had positive effects on such medical problems as drug abuse, alcoholism, depression, cancer, high blood pressure, and heart disease. A study underway with 4,000 elderly women has yielded preliminary results showing that people who attend church are both physically healthier and less depressed. Haney concludes that "maybe doctors should write 'go to church' on their prescription pads." Well, maybe.

The medical researchers in the studies reported above developed the following hypotheses to explain their findings:

- Religion may have a placebo effect on the ill.

- Sick church-goers may get better help from their fellow worshipers.

- Religious people are less likely to smoke, drink, and have other unhealthy habits.
- Prayer and ritual may lower harmful stress hormones.
- Divine intervention actually occurs.

While modern physicians may hypothesize, Luke has no doubt that the road to peace and the road to spiritual health lie in trusting God's goodness and his power to heal the sin-sick soul. Luke reports that in Jesus' last act on the cross, he said, "Father, into your hands I commend my spirit" (23:46). And in the last glimpse Luke gives us of the disciples they have "returned to Jerusalem with great joy, and they were continually in the temple blessing God" (24:53). A good prescription indeed for religious health: Trust in the goodness of God.

****

In many ways, religious health comes close to spiritual health in Luke's understanding of the good news of Jesus. But, as we have seen throughout this study, for Luke, the physician-as-Gospel-writer, spiritual health embraces *every* element of human life. The promise is that those who hear and do the word of God, as manifested in what Jesus said and did, can expect a gift of divine power. That gift, the Holy Spirit, will come to the disciples in a remarkable event described in Luke's sequel, the Acts of the Apostles. Luke is confident that the Holy Spirit is the essential source of complete health for those ready to witness for Christ, and for those united with Christ through unconditional, saving faith.

Where does Luke leave the disciples? Waiting and praising God. No doubt their joy was built on expectation; no doubt they had questions about what lay in store.

CHAPTER 7

FURTHER STEPS
TO SPIRITUAL HEALTH

"Faith is not daydreaming,
it is decision making!"
—Robert Schuller

As we conclude this thematic study of the Gospel According to Luke, we can pose a few culminating questions about the good physician and his stated or implied prescriptions for spiritual health:

What Is Spiritual Health?

We of the twenty-first century have trouble with the notion of the spiritual. Our age is not only thoroughly scientific in its world view, it is increasingly technological. The empirical sciences and their applied technologies depend on a grasp of *things*. We are more comfortable with what we can see and touch and hear and feel than we are with ethereal and abstract realities like faith and spirit. The Holy Spirit is even more confounding to the contemporary mind. Maybe the complex abstractness of cyberspace will change all that.

Perhaps we can derive some comfort from the positive thinking of Norman Vincent Peale: "Religious faith may very well be considered a science, for it responds invariably to certain formulae. Perform the technique of faith according to the laws which have proved workable in human experience and you will always get a result of power." Much of Luke's Gospel is directed exactly at the possibility of discovering spiritual laws that release the power of the Holy Spirit in the lives of men and women. But access to that power depends on faith in Jesus as Savior, God's "only begotten Son" (John 3:16, NKJV).

If God is a verb (as Fuller has suggested) and God is love, then (as the science of logic tells us) love is a verb. Spiritual health is the power-full consequence of unleashing the miraculous energy of love—for friends, enemies, the sick and wounded "on the margin" in society, and for God. That is both the simplest and most difficult task in human experience. That is what Luke is focusing on as he shows the power of *pneuma*, the vital force of the Holy Spirit, at work in restoring health to body, mind, and character in all of the dimensions we have explored in this study.

If health is wholeness—the development of integrity and peace within the soul, the church and society—then spiritual health is the most important goal anyone can have. The good news from the physician-author of this "connected narrative" of Jesus' life and work is that God's Holy Spirit is available for those who know their need of God, who ask/seek/knock, and who keep open hearts and minds. Spiritual health is the condition of peace that comes to the soul educated by the Holy Spirit for loving service. The Holy Spirit is "the true riches." The only way to get such *real* wealth is by faith in Christ; the only way you can keep it is to give it away to others.

Were the Disciples Spiritually Healthy?

They would hardly make such a claim. Jesus alone was the exemplar of spiritual health, the only one who knew and did the word of God perfectly. He tried to show the disciples how to live a life characterized by peace, love, justice, humility, and oneness with God and man. He was without sin and resisted all temptations that might undermine his strength and rob him of health. He taught his disciples as much as they could possibly hope to understand about God's kingdom and God's hope for broken mankind. But the disciples were not always good students or good patients.

It might be more accurate to say that the disciples were on a path leading to spiritual health. They were learners in the kingdom and, as Jesus noted, "a pupil is not superior to his teacher." Jesus, the teacher, was the exemplar of spiritual health, but the disciples could not expect to have learned all they needed to know to come close to his perfection. And they were often slow learners, blind and deaf to the good news of spiritual truth. How often they forgot and how frequently they misunderstood! But gradually they learned to "hear and do" the word of God. What kept the disciples from becoming spiritually healthy? Some general human weaknesses, and some specific weaknesses of given individuals kept them from achieving maximum potential, even in Jesus' own presence.

The general weaknesses include their dull wits and short memories, their tendency to miss the main point because they focused on concrete details, and their lack of faith. Their all-too-human pathological fear kept them from bold acts of spiritual power. And so it is with us. Cullen Hightower said, "Faith is building on what you know is here so you can reach what you know is there." Yes, but our foundations are not usually rock-solid, our knowledge is a sometime thing, and our resolve to build lacks drive and conviction.

The specific weaknesses of disciples run the gamut of human sin and sickness. For Judas it was the blindness of a zealot who did not see Christ as the Prince of Peace; for Peter it was the passion that spoke before it thought; for Thomas it was the doubt that impeded action. So it went with each disciple uniquely impaired in the quest for spiritual health. And so it is with us. What keeps you from full participation in the kingdom?

All of us are incapacitated by human motives at odds with God's vision for the kingdom. Money, power, prestige, fame, security, possessions—these desires block the channels by which the Holy Spirit enters the soul and frees us to give, to love, to live. Like the disciples we can only keep struggling up the path to spiritual health, to eternal life, knowing that ultimately it is only by God's power that we make any progress at all and knowing that even our faith in Christ's saving love is a gift from God.

Where Do I Go from Here?

Hadden Robinson has observed that "the Bible does not provide a map for life—only a compass." There is no doubt that we will often make wrong turns, even with a Bible in our hands. The spiritual journey offers many opportunities for detours, and we often lose our bearings. A compass, after all, only points us in the general direction we should go. Robert Schuller has said, "Faith is decision making." Which roads we take are up to us. The book of Luke describes many roads, and almost all of them are winding, dangerous pathways with surprising and interesting and educational adventures for those who travel.

On the Jericho road, the good Samaritan encountered an opportunity for kindness and true neighborliness. He responded to the opportunity to help someone in need, regardless of the danger and inconvenience.

On the road to Jerusalem, Jesus met and healed a poor blind man and forgave a reviled tax collector, in spite of the unpopular reception of such acts of charity.

On the road to Emmaus, two disciples met the resurrected Jesus, but something kept them from seeing who it was. Perhaps it was a preoccupation with their own loss and grief. And yet the "stranger" stayed with them, and finally "their eyes were opened, and they recognized him."

Scott Peck, in *Further Along the Road Less Traveled*, also sees life as a spiritual journey. He draws this interesting conclusion:

> When we were banished from Paradise, we were banished forever....We cannot go back. We can only go forward.... To proceed very far through the desert, you must be willing to meet existential suffering and work it through.... [We must] accept the fact that everything that happens to us is designed for our spiritual growth (pp. 19-24).

As Peck sees it, "the journey of life is not paved in blacktop; it is not brightly lit, and it has no road signs. It is a rocky path through the wilderness.... But we do not have to make the journey alone" (pp. 13-14). That seems an accurate assessment.

Anyone who journeys toward spiritual health can find in Luke certain steps along the path, rocky though it may be. Here are some steps that Luke endorses:

Steps to Wellness

1. We have to admit we are ill.

2. We have to take responsibility for our illness.

3. We have to choose to be well.

4. We have to ask God to help.

5. We have to act—confessing our sins and embracing the Spirit-filled life of Christ.

Beyond the Gospel Narrative

For those who would see how the early church struggled—sometimes failing, sometimes succeeding—to live the Spirit-filled life and to build up the community of believers, Luke provides a Gospel sequel, the book of Acts. There he recounts the remarkable events of Pentecost as the Holy Spirit dramatically descends upon the waiting disciples: "And suddenly from heaven there came a sound like the rush of a violent wind, and it filled the entire house where they were sitting. Divided tongues, as of fire, appeared among them, and a tongue rested on each of them. And all of them were all filled with the Holy Spirit..." (2:1-4). So the Christian church was launched by Spirit power.

Peter, the first great Christian preacher, was empowered by the Holy Spirit to declare that Jesus, exalted now at God's right hand, ". . . having received from the father the promise of the Holy Spirit . . . has poured out this that you both see and hear" (2:33). In his inaugural sermon, he announced the requirements for initiation into the new church: "Repent, and be baptized every one of you, in the name of Jesus Christ so that your sins may be forgiven; and you will receive the gift of the Holy Spirit" (2:38). A simple message, a clear prescription—unmistakable steps toward spiritual health. But how difficult a journey for sinners.

In his book on the role and power of the Holy Spirit, *Spirit Life* (1998), Jerry Vines provides this useful summary:

> As you read through the rest of Acts, you will see the continuity of the Spirit's permanence. In the next twenty-six chapters, the Spirit of God is mentioned in sixteen of them. The disciples were filled with the Holy Spirit on several occasions (4:8, 31, etc.). People weren't just filled one time. They were filled many times. The Holy Spirit of God gave wisdom (Acts 6:10). The Holy Spirit called people into service (13:2, 24). The Holy Spirit encouraged people (Acts 9:31). The Holy Spirit guided people (Acts 11:12). In Acts 16 the Holy Spirit said to Paul, 'Paul, you can't go that way. Go this way.' The Holy Spirit will guide you in your life. He's right there. He'll be with you forever. If you will ask him, he will guide you and lead you in your decision (p. 44).

This "continuity of the Spirit's permanence" is the quality Luke saw as fundamental to God's ongoing work to mend broken lives and build a spiritual unity in the midst of a fragmented society.

In the lives and ministries of Peter and Paul, we contemporary Christians can follow the work of the Holy Spirit in the creation of Christ's church on earth. Particularly in the incredible personal experiences of Paul, we can see how powerfully the Holy Spirit can affect the inner life of even the most obstinate among us. The book of Acts depicts, in the lives and works of Peter and Paul, the ways in which the Holy Spirit created the *healthy* community of believers: the Christian Church. Health and wholeness are not for solitary Christians (an oxymoron!) but for Christians working together to spread the gospel to the ends of the earth. Luke's narrative in Acts shows exactly how the Holy Spirit worked through the disciples, including the apostle Paul (whom Luke traveled with for a time), to bring harmony and unity to *all* those who had a common bond—their faith in Christ. Acts and the letters of Paul tell believers how to have a *healthy* church.

In the epistles of Paul—the earliest accounts of the church and those who shaped its formation—the reader encounters a sinner transformed in every way by the extraordinary power of the Holy Spirit. Paul's astounding repentance and journey in the faith is literally an "on the road" experience on the way to Damascus. Indeed, his ability to see is also a literal recovery of lost sight following his personal encounter with the resurrected Jesus, a Jesus he had persecuted and hated with passion. In Paul's salvation from the self "dead in sins" we see what God can do for, and through, those who repent of their sins and gain "new life" through "grace." If Paul, why not *any* person?

In the Gospel of Luke, we encounter disciples who are so frequently portrayed by the good doctor as "spiritually impaired." They are dull of mind, hard of hearing, myopic. As we have seen, they have difficulty truly repenting, committing themselves totally to serving God, loving fellow humans (even enemies) unconditionally. Is it farfetched to think that Luke—Paul's traveling companion—could see in his friend what power the Holy Spirit might exhibit in men and women who gave themselves completely to the service of Christ? Such an exemplar of unreserved faith, love, and service was Paul, who called himself "chief among sinners."

What a life Paul lived as an apostle of Christ! What an example of spiritual health! Although legend has it that Paul was physically frail—a small, bowlegged, nearsighted missionary with a "thorn in the flesh" (perhaps malaria or even epilepsy)—he was an intellectual giant. More importantly, he was a spiritual giant. What was his credo? How did the Holy Spirit enable him to become a spiritually healthy person?

For Paul, faith in Christ was the key to salvation. Luke wrote about how men and women might open themselves to receive the Holy Spirit. He was convinced that the spiritually healthy person let the Holy Spirit into the heart and mind in order to become Spirit-filled. Paul's thought goes in a different sense. For him, the solution to the sin that led to dysfunction and death was to find new life *in* Christ. Through faith, the believer actually became one with Christ, baptized into the spiritual being of Christ himself. So he could say to the Christians in Ephesus that they were "believers incorporate in Christ Jesus" (1:1, NEB), and as such "were marked with the seal of the promised Holy Spirit" (1:14).

And in his letter to another church he could assure the Christians in Rome that:

> How can we who died to sin go on living in it? Do you not know that all of us who have been baptized into Christ Jesus were baptized into his death? Therefore we have been buried with him by baptism into death, so that, just as Christ was raised from the dead by the glory of the Father, so we too might walk in newness of life (Rom. 6:2-4).

Paul's own conversion led him to the conviction that "newness of life" was a gift from God, a gift that led from sin to salvation, from life in the flesh to life in the Spirit. This was the path to the resurrection reality of Christ which is eternal life. This was the path Paul marked for *all* believers, for "God shows no partiality" (Rom. 2:11).

In a way, Paul (like Luke) is also a physician prescribing steps and pathways to wholeness, health, peace, and life. These traveling partners learned much from each other about medicine for the soul of a sin-sick world; each gave directions for the journey toward salvation. From Paul, as well as Luke, the Christian can find the example of faith and obedience that equips us for the trip.

A Final Thought About Dr. Luke

Luke's Gospel takes Christians of all eras through the geographical mazes the soul must travel in the wilderness of human life—as we attempt to reach our destination: spiritual health.

We do not as Christians have a road map, but Luke's biblical principles give us a compass. We have framed some of these principles as "prescriptions," reflecting the medical perspective of Luke as he might have assessed humanity's need for spiritual medicine. In their own way, they may serve as sign-posts on the road to health. Yes, the way to spiritual health is difficult and painful, but along the road we will meet those who need our help and those who can help us live more exciting, productive, satisfying lives. Healthy Christians always live in community to form the healthy church. Jesus will meet us on the road and give us the directions we need. This is the road to salvation, the road to health and wholeness. The good news from Dr. Luke is that we do not have to—indeed, cannot—make the journey alone.

SELECTED BIBLIOGRAPHY

I. Commentaries on Luke

Barclay, William. *The Gospel of Luke* (Revised Edition). Philadelphia: The Westminster Press, 1975. A classic in Barclay's The Daily Study Bible series. This is one of the most readable and insightful of the commentaries.

Dean, Robert J. *Layman's Bible Book Commentary: Luke*. Nashville: Broadman Press, 1983. This is a straightforward and clear analysis and a good primer for teachers as well as laymen.

Liefeld, Walter L. *The Expositor's Bible Commentary: Luke*. Grand Rapids, MI: Zondervan Publishing House, 1984. A commentary with a stance of "scholarly evangelicalism" and an approach that is "grammatico-historical." The analysis of Greek terms is helpful to the serious Bible student.

Miller, Donald G. *The Layman's Bible Commentary: The Gospel According to Luke* (vol. 18). Atlanta: John Knox Press, 1959. Designed as "a concise, non-technical guide for the layman," this commentary provides sound interpretation using the Revised Standard Version of the Bible.

Morgan, G. Campbell. *Studies in the Four Gospels*. Old Tappan, NJ: Fleming H. Revell Company, 1927. A classic analysis with Morgan's personal perspective clearly in evidence. Useful for comparing Luke's message with the other gospels.

Vines, Jerry. *Spirit Life: Experiencing the Power, Excitement, and Intimacy of God's Shaping Hand*. Nashville: Broadman and Holman Publishers, 1998. This is a comprehensive study of the Holy Spirit with particularly useful analysis of the nature and work of the Holy Spirit in Luke and Acts. Many contemporary applications and anecdotes are provided.

II. Commentaries on Parables

Barclay, William. *And Jesus Said: A Handbook on the Parables of Jesus*. Philadelphia: The Westminster Press, 1970. An elaboration of the parables found in Barclay's commentary on Luke. Beautifully written prose.

Buttrick, George A. *The Parables of Jesus*. Grand Rapids, MI: Baker Book House, 1981. Fine essays by a highly respected scholar-preacher. Using texts from the American Standard Version of the Bible, Buttrick sees the human element as central to his analysis of parables.

Briscoe, D. Stuart. *Patterns for Power*. Glendale, CA: Regal Books Division, G/L Publications, 1979. A brief commentary on selected parables in Luke. Briscoe identifies "one basic secret as it speaks to one fundamental issue" and focuses on such singular parable concepts as "prayerfulness," "lovingness," and "richness."

Hunter, Archibald M. *The Parables Then and Now*. Philadelphia: The Westminster Press, 1971. A prolific writer on the New Testament, Hunter focuses on the meaning of the parables in the contemporary world.

Jeremias, Joachim. *Rediscovering the Parables*. New York: Charles Scribner's Sons, 1966. Jeremias attempts to go back to the oldest forms of the parables to recover what Jesus himself meant by them. A useful study in providing a context of Palestinian history and culture.

Lockyer, Herbert. *All the Parables of the Bible*. Grand Rapids, MI: Zondervan Publishing House, 1963. An ambitious study of more than 250 parables, Lockyer synthesizes much of the scholarship on parables available in the 1960s. An excellent resource for those who want several perspectives on any given parable.

Morgan, G. Campbell. *The Parables and Metaphors of Our Lord*. Old Tappan, NJ: Fleming H. Revel Company, 1943. Although old, this commentary on the parables has strongly argued interpretations and applications. Morgan carried on the preaching mission of Dwight Moody.

Ogilvie, Lloyd John. *Autobiography of God*. Ventura, CA: Regal Books Division, G/L Publications, 1981. A personal, contemporary style of writing with modern applications. This is an engaging analysis of parables focusing on what they say about God.

Seagran, Dan. *The Parables*. Wheaton, IL: Tyndale House Publishers, Inc. 1978. Organized around "kingdom parables" and "people parables," this readable text is aimed not at theologians but "those who work on Main Street." Good contemporary applications.

Trench, Richard C. *Notes on the Parables of Our Lord*. Grand Rapids, MI: Baker Book House, 1948. This "popular edition" of Trench's classic analysis is a clear and academically sound commentary for teachers.

III. References on Health

Borysenko, Joan. *Minding the Body, Mending the Mind*. Reading, MA: Addison-Wesley Publishing Company, 1987. A fascinating study by a Harvard Medical School researcher on the relationship of mind to physical health. A practical guide to integrating psychology, spirituality, and biology.

Cousins, Norman. *Healing Heart: Antidotes to Panic and Helplessness*. New York: W. W. Norton & Company, 1983. Cousins' personal story of his own recovery from a severe heart attack with recommendations for how to form an active partnership with physicians. Looks at the ways attitudes and emotions can affect health.

Eims, LeRoy. *The Basic Ingredients for Spiritual Growth*. Wheaton, IL: Victor Books, 1992. A practical guide for spiritual growth, this text offers advice for achieving "a healthy, Christ-centered, spirit-controlled life."

Eyre, Linda and Richard. *Teaching Your Children Values*. New York: A Fireside Book, Simon and Schuster, 1993. An excellent and insightful guide for parents looking for ways to promote moral health for their children.

Hales, Dianne and Robert. *Caring for the Mind: The Comprehensive Guide to Mental Health*. New York: Bantam Books, 1995. The 873 page guide is an impressive review of mental disorders of every kind. Although based on a wealth of medical research, the diagnoses and treatment discussions are quite readable with easy to use checklists of symptoms for the layman.

Jourard, Sidney M. *The Transparent Self*. New York: Van Nostrand Reinhold Company, 1964. An old text with an insightful discussion of "healthy personalities" and "inspiriting in human wellness."

Larson, Bruce. *There's a Lot More to Health Than Not Being Sick*. Garden Grove, CA: The Cathedral Press, 1981. A popular book that looks at the relationship of mind and body from a Christian perspective. Larson focuses on the Christian call to take responsibility for choices affecting wellness.

Moore, Thomas. *Care of the Soul*. New York: Harper Collins, 1992. An application of psychotherapy principles to the development of a healthy spiritual life. Moore has ideas for how to "tend the soul by living artfully."

Peck, M. Scott. *The Road Less Traveled: A New Psychology of Love, Traditional Values, and Spiritual Growth*. New York: Simon and Schuster, 1978. A remarkable assessment of the spiritual and psychological connections required for growth of the integrated self. This book was on The New York Times bestseller list a record ten years.

_____. *Further Along the Road Less Traveled: The Unending Journey Toward Spiritual Growth*. New York: Simon and Schuster, 1993. In an equally remarkable sequel, Peck found to his "absolute horror" that he had become an evangelist. This book applies Peck's new-found Christian faith to the process of spiritual growth and health.

Rollins, Wayne G. *Jung and The Bible*. Atlanta: John Knox Press, 1983. Rollins explores "what it means to look at Scripture as a soul book..., as a treasury of the soul." He also examines the relationship of Carl Jung's psychological principles to biblical interpretation.

Siegel, Bernie S. *Love, Medicine, and Miracles*. New York: Harper and Row, Publishers, 1990. A physician's discovery that unconditional love is the most powerful stimulant of the immune system. Seigel found that exceptional patents who had the courage to love were the most likely to overcome disease.

Sheehan, M.D., David V. *The Anxiety Disease*. New York: Bantam Books, 1983. An interesting analysis of anxiety and its seven stages from "spells" to "depression." Sheehan discusses ways to manage recovery and re-establish mental health.

IV. Teachers' Resources

Canfield, Jack and Mark Victor Hansen. *Chicken Soup for the Soul: 101 Stories to Open the Heart & Rekindle the Spirit*. Deerfield Beach, FL: Health Communications, Inc., 1993. This book and its 1995 sequel *A 2nd Helping of Chicken Soup for the Soul* contain a wealth of essays, short stories, incidents, and poems that can serve as practical applications of Biblical principles.

Fulghum, Robert. *All I Really Need to Know I Learned in Kindergarten*. New York: Villard Books, 1988. This and other Fulghum books provide unusual perspectives on life's common events and puzzling mysteries. His essays can be used to illustrate Biblical principles in everyday life.

Griggs, Donald. *Basic Skills for Church Teachers*. Nashville: Abingdon Press, 1985. A good, short, practical primer for beginning teachers.

Groome, Thomas. *Christian Religious Education: Sharing Our Story and Vision*. San Francisco: HarperSan-Francisco, 1980. A fine text with a well-developed philosophy of Christian education.

Osmer, Richard Robert. *Teaching For Faith: A Guide for Teachers of Adult Classes*. Louisville: Westminster/John Knox Press, 1992. A well-written text for church teachers. Osmer outlines principles of teaching by lecture, discussion, life stories—and his chapter on the role of paradox is especially helpful for teaching parables.

Palmer, Parker. *To Know As We Are Known: Education As a Spiritual Journey.* San Francisco: HarperSanFrancisco, 1993. A literate and thoughtful reflection on how to develop spiritual health by living lives of truth and commitment.

Purdy, John. *Returning God's Call: The Challenge of Christian Living*. Louisville: Westminster/John Knox Press, 1989. A particularly good guide to help Christians apply Biblical precepts to social and community needs.

Van Ekeren, Glenn. *The Speaker's Sourcebook: Quotes, Stories and Anecdotes for Every Occasion*. Englewood Cliffs, NJ: Prentice Hall, 1988. This anthology and its 1994 sequel *Speaker's Sourcebook II* are a wonderful treasury of quotations, stories, and statistics—arranged by topic.

Walker, Robert Martin. *Politically Correct Parables*. Kansas City, MO: Andrews McMeel Publishing, 1996. This is a humorous (and contemporary) perspective on selected parables, including "The Geographically Dislocated Sheep," "The Generosity-Gifted Samaritan," and "The Ethically Impaired Stewperson." Such adaptations are useful attention-getters for a serious study of parables.

ᏮREAT BOOKS TO ENRICH YOUR LIFE!

What the Church Owes the Jew
~Leslie B. Flynn

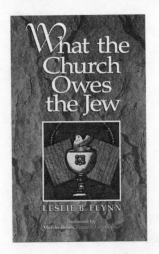

What do you know about the unique Jewish contribution to the Scriptures, the Church, and to the world at-large? Dr. Leslie Flynn, who served as pastor to many Jewish Christians in the New York area, passionately shares these answers and more (e.g., anti-Semitism, the Jewishness of Jesus), to help Jews and non-Jews build bridges of under-standing and friendship.
ISBN 0-9654806-3-1 paper $12.00

Positive Attitudes for the 50+ Years:
How Anyone Can Make Them Happy & Fulfilling
~Willard A. Scofield

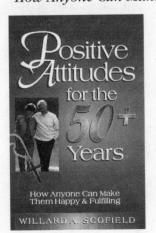

Looking for answers to some of the uncertainties of the 50+ Years? Willard Scofield, former associate editor for *Decision* magazine, and a Peale Center Guidance Counselor, shares insights to 75 often asked questions. Whether you have spiritual, financial, personal, relational, or other questions, you will find the answers in this help-ful, biblically-based handbook.
ISBN 0-9654806-2-3 paper $12.00

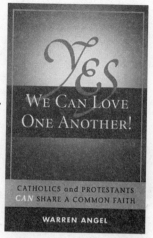
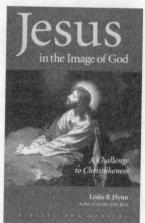

Why God Lets People Suffer
~Nancy C. Gaughan

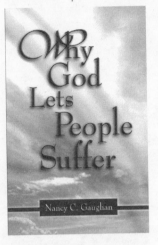

How can a God of love allow suffering in the lives of his people?
Having experienced much suffering in her childhood and adult years, Nancy Gaughan shares her discovery in the Scriptures of God's reasons for allowing suffering in the lives of his people. It is her conviction that even in suffering's worst moments we can know joy and faith and trust in the God who loves us.
ISBN 0-9654806-5-8 paper $12.95

Canine Parables
~Paulette Zubel

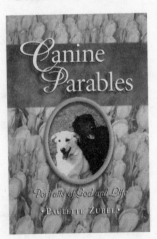

Can God's creatures teach us about him?
Paulette Zubel emphatically says, "Yes!" By observing her dogs' wacky and winsome antics, she reflects, through 63 devotionals, God's loving nature and our relationship with him. The old saying, "a dog is man's best friend," gets a new twist in *Canine Parables*. Paulette's dogs remind us that *God* is our best friend.
ISBN 0-9654806-4-X paper $12.95